Budget and Invest to

# Financial

# Freedom

A Guide to Budgeting, Credit Card
Churning, Risk-Free Investment,
Low-Risk Investment, Being a
Minimalist, Stocks, Bonds and Real
Estate

By Christopher Kent

# Table of Contents

INTRODUCTION ........................................................................ VI

CHAPTER ONE: WHO IS THIS BOOK FOR? ......................................... 1
OBTAIN FINANCIAL FREEDOM ......................................................... 1
Your current position ............................................................. 2
Positive attitude .................................................................. 3
Your goals ......................................................................... 4
Tracking your spending ........................................................... 5
Paying yourself first .............................................................. 5
Spending less ..................................................................... 6
Experiences instead of things .................................................... 7
Paying off your debts ............................................................. 8
Additional streams of income .................................................... 9
Investing in your future ......................................................... 10
HOW TO INVEST YOUR SAVINGS ..................................................... 11
Stocks ............................................................................ 11
Bonds ............................................................................. 11
Options ........................................................................... 12
Investment funds ................................................................. 12
Bank products .................................................................... 12
Retirement ....................................................................... 12
Annuities ......................................................................... 13
Alternative products ............................................................. 13
Mutual funds ..................................................................... 14
Commodity Futures ............................................................... 15
MEASURING AND KNOWING YOUR RISK TOLERANCE .............................. 15
Aggressive risk tolerance ....................................................... 16

CHAPTER TWO: HOW TO START BUDGETING ..................................... 20
ABOUT BUDGETING ................................................................ 20
STEPS TO FOLLOW ................................................................ 22
Identify the reason for creating a budget ....................................... 24
Retirement ....................................................................... 25
Savings ........................................................................... 28
Emergency fund .................................................................. 28
Cash envelopes ................................................................... 29
Fixed expenses ................................................................... 30
Variable expenses ................................................................ 30
SAVE MORE ........................................................................ 32
Small saving goals ............................................................... 32
Short term investments .......................................................... 34
Employers saving/retirement plans .............................................. 34

# Budget and Invest to Financial Freedom

*24-hour rule* ........................................................................... *35*
*Treat and save* ........................................................................ *35*
*Cost in value of hours worked* .............................................. *36*
CREDIT CARD ............................................................................ 36
*Eliminating your credit card debt* ......................................... *39*
DEBT CONSOLIDATION ............................................................. 41
*Debt Consolidation Agency* .................................................. *42*
*DSA- Debt Settlement Agency* .............................................. *43*
REFINANCE YOUR HOUSE ......................................................... 44
LOAN AGAINST YOUR VEHICLE ................................................. 44
SAVE ON YOUR UTILITY COSTS ................................................. 45

**CHAPTER THREE: BECOMING A MINIMALIST** ..........................**47**
BENEFITS OF MINIMALISM ....................................................... 47
*Prioritizing your spending* ................................................... *47*
*Reduces your need for things* ............................................... *48*
*You will need less* ................................................................. *48*
*Helps focus* ........................................................................... *49*
*Clear your debts* ................................................................... *49*
*Sell what you don't need* ...................................................... *50*
*Simplification of your finances* ............................................. *50*
*Giving becomes easier* .......................................................... *50*
BECOME A FINANCIAL MINIMALIST ......................................... 51
*Consolidating your bank accounts* ....................................... *51*
*Reduce your paperwork* ........................................................ *51*
*Number of credit cards* ........................................................ *52*
*No debts* ............................................................................... *52*
*Investing* ............................................................................... *53*
*Reduce your expenses* ........................................................... *53*
*Paying cash* ........................................................................... *54*
*No unnecessary services* ....................................................... *55*
*Restrict your goals* ................................................................ *55*
*Increase your income-generating activities* ......................... *56*
*Too much information* ........................................................... *56*

**CHAPTER FOUR: WHEN MUST I INVEST?** ...............................**57**
SHOULD I INVEST IF I HAVE STUDENT LOAN? ........................... 57
*Compound interest* ............................................................... *58*
*Tax deductions* ..................................................................... *59*
*List your priorities* ................................................................ *60*
IS 401K SUFFICIENT FOR RETIREMENT? ................................... 61
*Taxes and inflation* ............................................................... *62*
*Other fees and costs* ............................................................. *63*
*Lack of liquidity* .................................................................... *64*

# Budget and Invest to Financial Freedom

SETTING UP AN EMERGENCY FUND .................................................. 65
   *How much must you save for emergencies?* ............................ 65
   *Steps to build an emergency fund* ....................................... 67

**CHAPTER FIVE: RISK-FREE INVESTMENT ..................................... 70**
   BANK SAVINGS .......................................................................... 72
   ZERO COUPON BONDS .............................................................. 74
   GOVERNMENT BONDS .............................................................. 75
   CERTIFICATE OF DEPOSIT .......................................................... 77
   MONEY MARKET FUNDS ............................................................ 79
   INVESTMENT IN DIVIDEND SHARES .............................................. 80
   WARRANTS ............................................................................... 80

**CHAPTER SIX: LOW-RISK INVESTMENT ........................................ 83**
   CORPORATE BONDS .................................................................. 83
     *Corporate Bond Debt Funds* ........................................... 83
     *Who must invest in a Corporate Bond?* ............................ 84
     *Benefits and Features of a Corporate Bond* ..................... 84
     *Risk Factors and Returns* ................................................ 86
     *How Do Corporate Bonds Make Returns?* ........................ 87
     *Types of Corporate Bonds* .............................................. 87
     *Points to Remember* ...................................................... 88
   PREFERRED STOCKS .................................................................. 89
     *Features of Preferred Shares* ........................................... 89
     *Types of Preferred Stocks* ............................................... 91
     *Advantages of Preferred Shares* ...................................... 91
   ANNUITIES ............................................................................... 93
     *The Big Picture* .............................................................. 93
     *Tax Benefits of Annuities* ............................................... 94
     *The Bottom Line* ............................................................ 95

**CHAPTER SEVEN: HIGH-RISK INVESTMENT .................................. 97**
   INVEST IN OPTIONS .................................................................. 98
   SECURITIZATION ...................................................................... 99
   EXCHANGE-TRADED COMMODITY OR ETCS .............................. 101
   HEDGE FUND ......................................................................... 102
   STRUCTURED PRODUCTS ......................................................... 103
   ANGEL INVESTOR ................................................................... 106

**CONCLUSION .......................................................................... 108**

# INTRODUCTION

I want to thank you for choosing this book, *'Budget and Invest to Financial Freedom - A Guide to Budgeting, Credit Card Churning, Risk-Free Investment, Low-Risk Investment, Being a Minimalist, Stocks, Bonds and Real Estate.'* I am sure you will have a completely different perspective about your finances once you have finished reading it.

Do you want to attain financial freedom, but aren't sure where to start? If yes, then this is the perfect book for you. The reason you have chosen this book is either your finances are in terrible shape, or you foresee some financial difficulties and want to know how to prevent these or just plan for a hassle-free retired life. Either way, I am sure this book will help you.

In this book, you will learn about the basics of budgeting, steps to start budgeting, tips to attain financial freedom, setting your financial goals, understanding your financial position, steps to opt for a minimalistic lifestyle, and much more. Apart from this, you will also learn about the different types of investments according to the risks involved while investing in them. By using the information given in this book, you can see a positive change in your financial position.

So, if you are ready to learn more about all of this, then let us get started without further ado!

# CHAPTER ONE

# WHO IS THIS BOOK FOR?

## Obtain Financial Freedom

Financial freedom is something that everyone wants, and the good news is, anyone can attain it. I mean anyone; even those who have student debt can attain financial freedom. As is obvious from the phrase, financial freedom is about having sufficient funds and a dependable cash flow that lets you live the kind of life you want. Regardless of any financial troubles that you might have today, you can always work to attain financial freedom. You don't have to worry about paying any bills or bearing any sudden expenses. Also, your debt burden is non-existent once you attain financial freedom. In this section, you will learn about the different tips that you can follow to attain financial freedom.

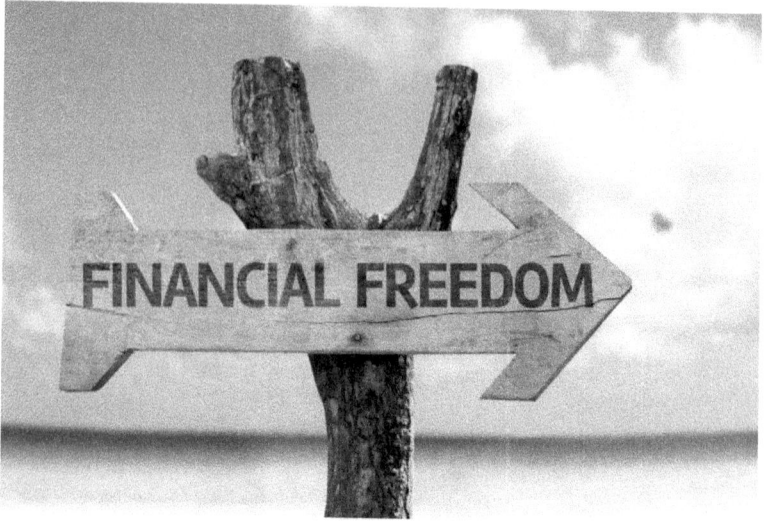

## *Your current position*

You cannot attain financial freedom if you are not aware of your existing financial position. Working out your finances, especially acknowledging your debt, your savings, and the money you need, might not be a pleasant activity. However, this is something that needs to be done to start working in the right direction. You need to make a list of all the debts you have like mortgages, car loans, credit card bills, student loans, or any other debts. You must also include any money you owe your friends or family members. Regardless of how small the debt might be, you must make a note of it. Please be realistic while estimating your debts.

Once you make a list of all your debts, take a deep breath. This is a step in the right direction. How much is your total debt? Don't worry even if the number seems to be slightly on the higher side. The next step is to look at your savings. Include all the different forms of savings you have like savings account in the bank, stocks, any retirement fund, insurance, and such. Then, you need to add your source of monthly income like salary and any additional income you receive. Keep these numbers handy as you go through the other steps discussed in this chapter.

Phew, that's one thing out of the way.

## *Positive attitude*

Debt can make you feel disappointed and even discouraged. However, please remind yourself that money is a good thing, even if it does seem to place a lot of burden on you at this moment. You need to ensure that you maintain a positive attitude toward money. Keep reminding yourself that with the right investment strategy and savings, you can easily attain the financial freedom you want.

A lot of people don't earn as much as they want because of the shame that is associated with making money. Money is an important part of your life, and you cannot do away with it. However, the real trouble starts when you start loving money more than anything else. Money isn't the root of all evil, but the love of money is. So, you need to ensure that you have a positive attitude toward money. You need to understand that money is like any other necessity in life, such as food or water. It helps you acquire the things you need. If you want financial freedom, then you must ensure that you start viewing money as a quintessential tool, which will help you attain your goals. If you have a negative attitude about money, your subconscious might try to sabotage your progress.

## *Your goals*

Now that you know money is not evil, what do you need money for? Are there any specific goals you wish to attain? You might want to pay off your debts and start afresh. You might want to quit your regular job and enjoy an early retirement, or maybe you want to follow your passions. You might want to create a retirement fund or maybe save for a rainy day.

Regardless of what your reasons are, it is advised that you must make a note of all your goals. It is quite an enriching and enthralling experience to watch the progress you make toward attaining your goals. If you are trying to pay off all your debts, then it is quite motivating to watch your debts diminish while your savings increase. Every step in the right direction gives you the motivation to keep going.

However, if you don't have any goals, you will not be able to measure your progress. Also, if you want to have a sense of direction, then you need to have goals. Once you make a list of your goals and keep referring to it daily, your subconscious also starts to encourage you to work toward the end result you want. While setting goals, you must ensure that they are specific, measurable, reasonable, attainable, and time bound. If a goal doesn't meet all these criteria, then it is not a good goal. For instance, you can have a goal to pay off $24,000 of student loans within the next six months. This is a specific goal, which is attainable and time bound. If you set unattainable goals for yourself, you are merely setting yourself up for disappointment.

If you are aware of what you need to achieve, achieving it certainly becomes easier.

## *Tracking your spending*

You need to start tracking your spending if you want to attain financial freedom. You can use a different online tool like Mint to keep track of your spending and your expenses. You can also set monthly budgets for each category of expenses and see whether you can stick to the budget or not. By doing this, you will not only get a realistic picture of your monthly expenses but will also become conscious of your spending. Once you are aware of how much you spend and how you spend it, it becomes easier to cut back on expenses and spending. I suggest that you start using an app or an online tool to track your monthly expenses. Becoming conscious of your spending is the best way to start budgeting.

## *Paying yourself first*

You might have come across the phrase "pay yourself first." If you haven't, don't worry. It essentially means that you must first save a specific sum before you can start paying for anything else. You need to pay yourself first to increase your savings. It is believed to be one of the simplest ways to create a savings for yourself. Why do you need to do this? For instance, if you set aside $1000 the instant you get your salary, then regardless of what you do with the rest, you will have $1000 as savings by the month end. If you run short of funds, then you will probably need to come up with alternative sources of income to make up for other costs.

When you start to pay yourself first, you are essentially making sure that you will always have some funds to invest in yourself. If you don't do this, your savings will never be fixed, and it is quite likely that you will only end up saving whatever you are left with at the end of the month. If you want to have substantial savings, then you must make it a point to pay yourself first. There are other ways in which you can start investing in yourself. For instance, if your employer offers a retirement savings program, then you can set up an automatic payment option where a fixed sum is deducted from your salary every month and is deposited in your retirement fund. By doing this, you can make sure that you don't neglect your responsibility of saving for the future.

### *Spending less*

Did you know that Warren Buffet purchased a house for $31,500 in 1958 and has been staying there ever since? Given that he is one of the richest men alive today, he still lives in the same house. He can certainly afford the best the world has to offer, but, at times, frugality is important. On the other hand, Kanye West loves to flaunt his money to the extent that he once had debt worth millions of dollars. Both of these gentlemen are quite successful and rich. The only difference is that one of them didn't spend more than he needed, and it helped increase his riches.

By spending less, you can ensure that you get richer. For instance, you have $1,000 set aside for expenses. You usually spend $800 and save $200. However, if you cut back on your expenses and spend only $500, your savings will increase, and you will be able to save $500.

## *Experiences instead of things*

This point ties back to the one listed above. Life is certainly short, and it is not about hoarding money until you are in your sixties. In your bid to save, you must not forget about living and enjoying your life. Remember that by forgetting to live, it ultimately defeats the purpose of even saving. Ultimately, the things that will ensure that you had a happy and fulfilling life are all the experiences you have along the way and not the things you own. Take a moment and think about it. The happiness you get from the things you buy is it momentary or everlasting? Does the debt created from your purchases make things easier for you? Now, it is time to rethink all this. What is your happiest memory? What were you doing and who were you with? The focus of your life must be about creating more happy memories instead of collecting materialistic things.

You might have always dreamt about traveling to Greece and might have been saving up to do this. So, go on your dream vacation and don't feel guilty about it. You didn't incur a debt to do something you wanted. Life consists of little moments like this that tend to make you happy. The best times you ever have come from spending time with your loved ones. So, it is time to rethink what happiness means to you, and it is time to concentrate on doing the thing you love.

Also, you don't have to spend the money you don't have to keep up the pretense that you do have money.

## *Paying off your debts*

Some people might think that it is better to invest your money instead of paying off any debts. Unless you are a seasoned stock trader who always makes a profit on all your trades, it is highly unlikely that you will be able to clear your debts by making more investment. Incurring a debt will be a reason for unnecessary stress, regardless of whether you realize this or not. As soon as you clear your debts, you will certainly feel quite relieved. If you have a debt of $20,000 and have about $15,000 in the bank, you will still not be considered to be debt-free until you pay off the entire amount. Clearing your debts is certainly not a glamorous way to spend your money. However, by paying off your debts, you will be a step closer to attaining financial freedom.

The two methods of debt repayment you can opt for our snowball and avalanche. In the avalanche method, you will essentially be paying off those loans with the highest rate of interest, whereas in the snowball method, you will need to pay off the smaller debts before clearing other debts. You must decide which of these methods will work best for you. If you have multiple debts, then the snowball method might be ideal. When you can see for yourself that your debts are being cleared one after the other, it gives you the motivation to keep going. Even paying off the smallest of debts can make you feel quite good about yourself.

Paying off any debts will make you feel like a huge weight is taken off your shoulders. After you pay off the debts, you can steadily see an increase in your savings. If you clear your debts, then you can increase your savings. You can always invest even when you have debts. However, you must learn to be smart about the way you go about it.

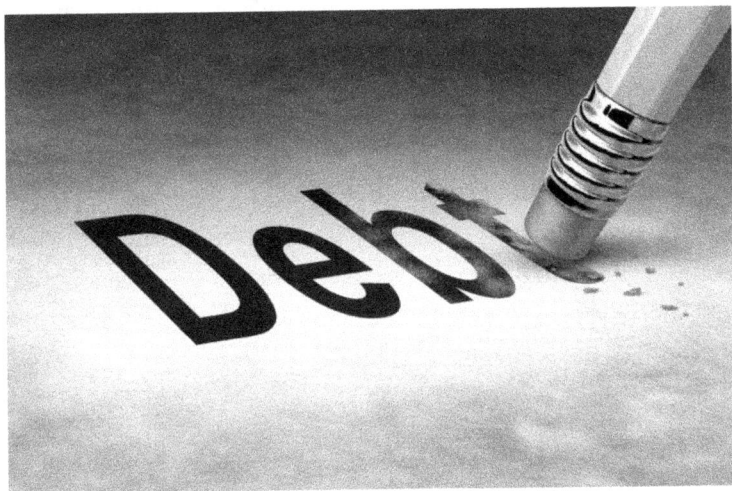

## *Additional streams of income*

Here is a common question that a lot of people seem to keep wondering about- "How can I ever clear my debts when I don't have sufficient income?" If you want to attain financial freedom, then you must realize that it will take time and effort. Your regular 9-5 job might not help you earn sufficient income to pay off your debts as well as monthly expenses. So, if that's the case, then it is time to consider additional sources of income to help attain your financial goals. There are two primary sources in which you can earn more - active and passive income. Active income refers to an activity like trading whereas a passive source of income is one, which keeps the income flowing with minimal effort. If you want to trade daily, then your work will be limited to only a couple of hours per day. You can become a freelance writer, a virtual assistant, pick up any jobs on Craigslist, or even become an Uber driver. You can opt for an active stream of income if you know that you will have sufficient time in the day to work on your other sources of income apart from your regular job.

If you are certain that you will not be able to devote much time, then it is time to look at passive income ideas. You can start a drop shipping business, customized items store, sell content online, rent out your property, or even become an affiliate marketer. You can use your skills to help you earn a nice additional source of income.

## *Investing in your future*

Well, this might be the last tip in this section, but it is quite important. If you follow all the advice give up until now, then you will be debt free and might have also started to save some funds. Doing this might help increase your financial health at the moment. However, what will you do if there is an emergency to attend to? It is quite important that you create a fund for a rainy day. You must start investing in your future. You need to create a retirement fund to support your lifestyle post-retirement. You can easily make monthly contributions from your salary account toward investing in your future.

You not only must save for your retirement, but you must also start creating an emergency fund. You never know when an emergency might present itself, and you must have sufficient funds to deal with the emergencies that come your way. You will learn more about creating an emergency fund in the subsequent chapters.

## How to Invest Your Savings

There are different options available you can use when thinking about investing to meet your financial goals. Each type of investment has different benefits as well as drawback and opportunities. In this section, you will learn about the different types of investment to make the most of your savings.

### Stocks

Whenever you purchase any stocks in a company, you become a part owner of the company. There are different types of stocks you can invest in, and they are usually categorized according to the size of the company, type, the term of growth, and the way the stock performs during a given market cycle.

### Bonds

A loan that an investor gives an organization is referred to as a bond. The company needs to pay the investor timely interest on the bond while the principal on the date of maturity of the bond remains unchanged. Different types of bonds include corporate, treasury, agency, and muni bonds.

## Options

Essentially, options are contracts that offer the buyer a right to buy or sell the underlying stock, exchange-traded fund, or any other security at a specific price before the expiry date of the option. Options only offer a preferential right and aren't an obligation by any means.

## Investment funds

Different funds like mutual funds, exchange-traded funds, and closed-end fund are types of investment funds. When it comes to funds, people tend to collect money from different investments and then invest those funds based on an investment strategy. Funds not only offer diversification of your investment portfolio but also allow for different types of investment strategies and styles. However, not all funds are created equally.

## Bank products

Banks, along with credit unions, offer a convenient and safe way to accumulate your savings. Some banks and other financial institutions even offer services that can help manage your funds effectively. Checking or savings accounts lend flexibility and liquidity to your funds. Apart from this, a savings account also offers an annual interest on the funds placed within the savings account.

## Retirement

There are various types of investments that are available if you want to save for your retirement. Not just that, you have different instruments available, which help to manage your income post retirement. For instance, a 401k is a retirement savings option which offers certain tax concessions or maybe an IRA. Managing your retirement income and saving for your retirement is an effective and necessary investment that you must make if you want financial security.

## Annuities

A contract that exists between the holder of the instrument and an insurance company is referred to as an annuity. The company essentially starts to make either periodic payments or agrees to pay a specific sum at a pre-agreed time in the future. Annuities can be deferred or immediate annuities.

## Alternative products

Alternative and complex products like notes which include principal protection or even high-yield bonds, tend to offer great returns. However, the risk associated with such instruments is quite high when compared to conventional forms of investment. When it comes to investing, the greater is the risk, the higher is the payout. There are different ways to invest apart from the ones that have been mentioned so far. A few of these investments have been discussed below. Investments in real estate can be made by purchasing commercial or residential property. There are REITs (real estate investment trusts) that pool together the investor's money and acquire properties. These REITs are traded just like stocks. Mutual funds and ETFs also invest in REITs. Private equity as well as hedge funds are classified as alternative investments. However, these options are available to those who meet the specifications regarding income and net worth. Private equity also allows the companies to raise the necessary capital without having to go public.

## *Mutual funds*

This is a pooled investment and it is managed by an investment manager. It allows the investors to have their money invested in various stocks, bond, or other types of investment as has been stated in the prospectus of the mutual fund. These instruments are valued at the end of a trading day. All the transactions regarding the buying and selling of shares are to be executed after the market closes. Mutual funds can be actively or passively managed. Those that are actively managed tend to be costlier. Distributions can be made in the form of dividends, interest, and capital gains as well. These distributions of mutual funds are subject to taxation. Just like with stocks or bonds, selling a mutual fund can result in a profit or a loss. A mutual fund allows a small investor to acquire a diversified exposure to a number of investment holdings that fall within the purview of such an investment. Mutual funds allow an investor, big or small, to achieve some diversification in their investments instantly.

## *Commodity Futures*

A commodity future is an agreement to buy or sell a fixed quantity of a commodity at an agreed price on a specific date in the future. Commodities can include metals, oils, animal products, grains, financial instruments, and currency too. Trading in commodity futures contracts usually takes place at commodity exchanges. Federal regulations allow the trade of futures contracts on single stocks and are known as single stock futures and security indices.

Insurance

There are different kinds of life insurance products available like term life, universal life, and even whole life policies. There are also variations available in each of these options.

In the subsequent chapters, you will learn in detail about the different types of investment options available to diversify your investment portfolio and increase your savings.

## Measuring and Knowing Your Risk Tolerance

When it comes to calculating the return on investment, there are different variables at play. Your risk tolerance refers to your willingness and your ability to withstand any such variability. You must have a precise and realistic understanding of the risks you can and cannot tolerate. If you take on a risk that is too much for you to handle, then all it will do is end up giving you more stress. If you get in way over your head, it will defeat the purpose of investing. You must be aware of the risks you can take if you want to become a successful investor. Investing

# Budget and Invest to Financial Freedom

is not a gamble, especially because it involves your hard-earned money.

You can use a risk related questionnaire to assess your risk tolerance. You must consider various worst-case scenarios wherein your investments don't turn out like you hoped and the returns you get from them are disappointing. If the worst-case scenario comes true and you lose your investment, will you be able to tolerate the loss you incur? If you think you will not be able to tolerate such risks, then you need to reconsider the investments you want to make. There are several instruments to choose from when it comes to investing and you must opt for one that meets your needs without leaving you vulnerable to unnecessary risks.

There are various factors that influence your risk tolerance like your future earnings, your current financial situation, other investments you have, and the timeframe within which you want to invest. When you have stable income to depend on, your tolerance for risk will be slightly higher than those who don't have a stable source of income. As long as you have the necessary funds available, you can take bigger risks. However, the risks you take must be calculated risks and not impulsive. The risk tolerance of an investor can be usually categorized as the following.

## *Aggressive risk tolerance*

Aggressive investors are usually well versed with the conditions prevailing in the market. They have a grasp of how securities function. The knowledge they possess is the main reason why they can invest in high-risk investments and come out as winners. High-risk investments like becoming an angel investor or investing in a venture capital funds is quite risky as the name suggests because of the volatility of such options. Investing in the securities of a company whose value can plummet to zero without any warning or expensive options, which become worthless upon maturity are volatile investments. An aggressive investor will certainly have no qualms about investing in high-risk instruments as long as the returns offered by it are sizeable. For instance, in 2014, David Einhorn of Greenlight capital valued the shares of SunEdison at $32 per share. He went ahead and invested about $480 million in that company. Due to some fraudulent accounting and other malpractices, the price of those shares plummeted to 14 cents per share in 2016. Well, that was quite a nosedive and the investor was left to bear the brunt of the crash. As mentioned, higher the risk, the higher is the payout. Well, this is possible only when things go as planned. If there are any deviations in the performance of the investment, then the risk of loss is quite significant. So, don't just jump into investing in high-risk investments if you aren't prepared to shoulder any losses.

**Moderate risk tolerance**

A moderate investor is someone who doesn't mind taking up risky investments, as long as they are combined with some risk-free or low-risk investments. They believe in equally spreading the risk across their investment portfolio. The most common strategy an investor with moderate risk-tolerance will opt for is one where 50% of his portfolio consists of high-risk investments and the rest is made up of low-risk or no-risk investments. This not only helps to mitigate any losses, but also helps to spread the risk across a variety of instruments.

**Conservative risk tolerance**

All those investors who opt for a conservative approach to investing will want to invest in assets that aren't volatile. A conservative investor will look for such investments that offer security along with liquidity. These investors usually opt for low-risk or no-risk investments. This is a good game plan, especially if you are in it for the long haul. Savings accounts, certificates of deposit, Treasury bills, and other money market instruments are the ideal options for a conservative investor. You will need to gauge your willingness to take risks. Depending on your ability to stomach risks, you can select the instrument accordingly.

To understand your risk tolerance, you need to analyze your financial health. You will learn more about this in the subsequent chapters.

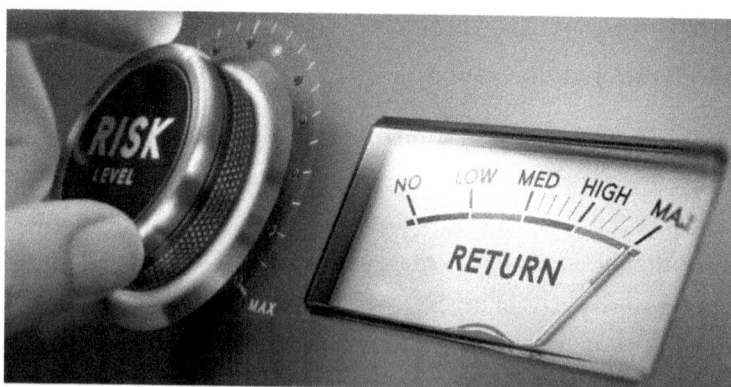

# CHAPTER TWO

# HOW TO START BUDGETING

## About Budgeting

All of us lead a hectic lifestyle and have no time to "stand and stare" or just grab a breather, so in such situations, very few make time to plan out a budget. This, however, is very important and, if you have browsed through for any financial advice on how to make ends meet, by now you will know that there is one simple rule that pops up in every piece of advice. You need a budget. Budget, in a nutshell, is a plan to make sure your hard-earned income meets not only your day-to-day needs but also helps to prepare for unseen contingencies. Once you have a budget in place, you have pre-assigned your money for specific tasks, and that ensures you spend your money wisely. What it also does is let you see where you are leaking money due to unwanted expenses and helps you determine which expenses can either be reduced or even stopped in their tracks.

As with everything else, forming a habit is always useful, and preparing a budget helps you with your spending habits, and that is the first step toward making your money work more efficiently for you.

The very thought of creating a budget will put thoughts in your mind that it will be a complicated procedure, and whether you will be able to create one or not. Initially even with simple step by step guidelines it may seem difficult but no good was ever easy to achieve, so roll up those sleeves, and after some initial hard work, it will become a habit and then just follow the step by step guidelines provided in this book, and you will find creating a budget a very simple exercise.

So, grab a pen and paper and let's get started, the very first thing you need to ask yourself is why you need a budget? It can be any one of the following reasons or more, note down your list of reasons.

- Finding a way to save more money.
- Reduce unwanted expenses.
- Not having to argue with your spouse about money.
- Making sure your spending habits are in sync with your goals.
- Find a way to move out of the vicious paycheck-to-paycheck cycle.
- Avoiding buying things on credit (needs vs. wants)
- Getting out of existing debt.
- Creating a clear financial path for future financial goals.

## Steps to Follow

I am sure I have covered some if not all of your requirements, so let's move ahead to creating a budget.

The very first thing you will need to do is list down all your expenses however big or small they may be. It does not matter if it is a daily expense or a once a year expense, you need to write it all down. Initially, it is recommended you do this exercise for one whole month and list down every expense no matter what it is. This will then give you a picture of your spending habits. There are a couple of ways you can track this. The most basic of them all is to always carry a pen and a small notepad, and every time you reach for your card or cash, make an entry. Then, at the end of the day, fill all of it on a spreadsheet. This is a more hands-on approach and also time-consuming. Initially you might even miss a few entries, so start forming a habit of keeping all your receipts to do a back check. Also, initially you can take your card statements for the last couple of months and start by adding those entries in your spreadsheet. You may not remember every transaction or what it was for, but it will still give you a broad picture of your spending habits.

There are also several APPS online, which will help you, track your expenses, and you can download the one which suits you, and that will take care of tracking your expenses. It will require a one-time effort on your part to link all your cards and accounts to the app but once done, every swipe and every withdrawal will automatically be captured for your future reference.

You may be wondering what the point of this cumbersome exercise is. How is listing all my expenses going to help me? Believe it or not, it's going to be an eye-opener for you. Let's say I ask you; do you know how much you spend monthly on food or gas? Do you think you can give me an exact figure? Chance are you won't have a vague idea, but once the budget is in place, not only will you know where your money is going but what exactly you need to do to reduce wastage and leaks from your hard-earned money.

Now that you know how to go about tracking your daily expenses, grab a calendar and mark out all the important dates for the rest of the year. When I say important, I mean all dates where you may have to spend more than your regular daily budgeted expenses, they will be:

- Birthdays
- Gifting festivals like Christmas
- Annual premiums for your insurance
- Vacations if any planned
- Taxes and professional dues
- Annual medicals
- Car repair/maintenance
- Property taxes

And anything else that you know you will be spending in the upcoming year. To help, you can check your bank and card statements for the last twelve months if you have them. If not, request a copy and that will help you identify these expenses.

One more important thing. If you have a variable income, it will be difficult to plan a budget so what you will need to do in such a scenario is to pay yourself a monthly salary. The amount can either be your average for the year of if you want to be safe the least you have made in any month. That will give you a better cushion and reduce your risk of overspending.

## *Identify the reason for creating a budget*

Now that you have decided to make a budget, first let's find out why. It can be any one or all or more of the following reasons.

- You want to save for your retirement.
- You want to build a fund for emergencies
- You want to buy a house
- You want to buy your dream car
- You want to pay off your debt
- You want to save for college fees
- Plan a vacation

Once you have decided what your aim is, you can then customize your budget around your goals and how to achieve them. Studies have shown that setting goals helps increase your motivation and thereby increase your success rate. To be effective, you need to set absolute specific goals, like if you want to buy that dream car, it must be assigned a specific number as well like "need to save $15,000 by this date." Setting a deadline is also very important, so you know exactly how much you need to save every month toward that goal.

The more specific the targets are, the greater the chances of you succeeding, but if you have no predefined goals yet, you can decide on a random number like I will save 20% or 25% of my income and then use the same as and when required. However, based on thorough research, it has been found specific is terrific.

If you are not sure how much you need to save for retirement, college fees or how big a house you need to save for, we will be discussing this in detail in the coming chapters.

If you are single, then you are ready to start planning. However, if you are married, you need to ensure you discuss this with your partner. In some cases, there are instances where partners maintain separate finances. Even then, you will need to bring your partner on board as suddenly there may be a change in your spending habits, and your partner must be aware why. The same reason applies in case of combined finances, plus the fact that you will need to make it a team effort as you cannot stick to a plan and have your partner leaking money by spending outside of the budget.

There is no fixed order in deciding which task you need to budget first, so you can choose as per your priority all that needs to be budgeted from the detailed list below.

## *Retirement*

Let's start with retirement and how much you need to keep aside for your retirement. So, you will need to first arrive at a figure based on your living habits, how much you will need to save to provide yourself a stress-free retirement. To put a figure to your expenses, you will need to create a sample budget factoring in your current monthly expense, plus you need to consider if your mortgage will be paid off by then or not? Will you be traveling more, or will you be content with just relaxing? Will you be taking up some hobbies that will require you to invest some funds in them? Also, something very important for you to remember will be potential health issues that can pop up after retirement. Once you have factored all of the above into the equation, you will arrive at a figure that you need after retirement. You then need to take into account any active income that you may receive at that point and deduct that from the required amount.

To calculate the income, you will have coming in post your retirement you will need to factor in three key things

- Social security
- Pension plan from the employer
- Savings
- Source of income post retirement

Social security is one of the most common and primary sources of income for retirees, but having said that, as per the last survey, the average benefit is about $1350, so you do not want to rely on this source of income alone.

Less than 20% of private sector workers had a defined pension plan a few years back. So, if you are one of the few with this option available, you need to get in touch with your plan administrator and figure out exactly how much benefit you will be eligible for. The exact amount may not be possible as the amount may vary based on your total number of years of service plus your actual age at the time of retirement, but with the help of the administrator, you must be able to arrive at a workable figure for your budget. Also, a common mistake at this stage is that people factor in their investments in 401k, etc. but that will be wrong as you are trying to calculate what amount you need to invest in producing your desired income.

Now that you have calculated two of the three key things, what you now need to do is calculate the difference between what you are going to need post-retirement and what you will be earning from the top two options, the difference that you are left with will have to come from your savings. Having said that, the aim must be the savings must be in the form of investments, which will generate enough income to bridge the gap without you having to dip into your principal amount. If you can do that, you don't need to worry about running out of cash after you retire. Since your principal balance will remain the same while you manage your expenses on the income from your investments, the returns on the investments you make will also depend on a lot of factors though some investments may give high returns initially. They may not give the same returns after a few years if they are dependent on market fluctuations, so you will need to invest in something safe, something that may give you less returns but will remain steady irrespective of market conditions. The good part about this is you will be saving a higher principal amount to do that, and that would, in turn, give you a better safety cushion after your retirement.

The above option is the simple option but what if you cannot come up with enough savings to meet the safe investments options and create a safety net? In such scenarios, you need to create a disciplined plan where you dip into your principal amount and withdraw a fixed amount every year. To do this, give yourself 30 years of retirement and calculate the principal amount accordingly. You can calculate a minimum return on this investment and deduct that amount yearly.

However, with rising taxes, healthcare costs and other uncertainties, it is always a better idea to estimate a little more than you feel you will require, the only outcome of that being that you will reach a higher savings goal and be able to lead a more comfortable life or stay afloat in case there is an emergency.

## Savings

Now that you know your expenses and what it's going to take to have a life free of financial worries, let's start with saving. Unless you have money left over, you are not going to meet any of your targets so let's see how we can save some from your actual paycheck. Given below is a list of saving techniques in random order. You can choose whichever suits you the best.

## Emergency fund

Emergency fund, the name says it all; it is a fund that you are going to require in an emergency. It can be a medical emergency or a sudden loss of a job, unplanned travel, car troubles or any other emergency. So, the funds need to be easily accessible as well. Typically, the amount required in an emergency fund is 3-6 months of your monthly expenses. Once you have the number, the question is where to park the funds. Investing it can result in delay if you really need the cash in an emergency and just keeping it in your bank account can easily mean a swipe of your card and the fund is gone. It has to be a combination of both. To be safe, open a separate account with no add on facilities like debit card, or even online access. Also, make sure the bank is not too close to where you live, so if you need the funds, you might have to make a short trip, but yes, the funds will be there for you. How much of the 3-6 months back up funds you want to park in your account is up to you but keep at least some part in money market funds. A Mutual fund that invests in short term securities tends to have a low rate of return but, in return, what you get is fewer fluctuations. Also, the point of having an emergency fund is not to make money, but what's the harm if they're in an opportunity to earn some interest on your saved money.

## *Cash envelopes*

Now that you have created a budget and allocated limit for each category of your expenses, let's start with one of the basic methods, which will help you follow your plan and stick to, the limits set by you.

Please note it is very important to complete the planning stage of your budget diligently before you begin using the cash envelope system. You cannot just stuff cash in different envelopes for different expenses and expect the system to work. This step is to be used only after successful tracking of your expenses for at least a month along with backtracking of receipts wherever possible. You can, of course, tweak the amounts later but you need to arrive at a figure systematically and not just by guesswork. Once you have the figures in your budget, you will see there are two types of expenses - fixed expenses, and variable expenses.

## Fixed expenses

These are expenses in your monthly budget that never change. The value of these expenses will remain the same month on month; examples of fixed expenses will include the monthly installment on your car payment, your insurance premiums, and so on. These expenses must not be a part of your cash envelope as you cannot control these expenses, and they have to be paid off monthly.

## Variable expenses

All the rest of your expenses from your budget list need to be paid for using the cash envelope system. The best way to get started is to decide on the total figure you will need from your budget sheet and then on your payday go and withdraw that amount. You can add a small twist to this as well. Now that you know not just the total but the breakup of how much each envelope will require, make a list of the denominations that you will require as well to stuff those envelopes. Try and avoid smaller bills as it has been observed that while shopping people are generally reluctant to break a $50 or a $100 as compared to a $5 or $ 10. Anything that can help you save works, right!

The main reason for using cash envelopes is because it is so successful, as it is a visual system. You can see money flowing out, and your mind automatically starts to go into a saving mode. Many people do not overspend because they do not have the funds, but simply do it because they have no idea where the money is going. With a cash envelope, the moment the money starts reducing in your envelope, your spending automatically gets a bit tighter as you self-realize that you are overspending and once this money is gone, you cannot borrow from other envelopes. A classic example is when we go shopping. Most of us do not have a shopping list, and we grab what we like from the shelf and pay for it with a card. We do this without realizing what we purchase or how much we paid for it. However, with a cash envelope as you start billing and see the count steadily increasing and compare it with the money left in your envelope, the realization hits you that the money left will not be sufficient to meet your budget requirements. You will automatically put back unnecessary things like the magazine you picked up while waiting in line or the 12 pack of soda plus cookies etc. This visual aspect of watching your cash is a tremendous motivator to avoid unwanted purchases and help you buy what you need and not necessarily what you want.

Once you have stuffed your envelopes, you need to make sure that you only use each envelope for the purpose it was earmarked for. So, do not forget to either label every envelope with the category of funds or, if you want, you can get different colored envelopes to help you identify more easily what that envelope is for.

If the money in your envelope is used up and it isn't time to refill the envelope, then it can mean two things- either you didn't budget the right amount for a specific category of expenses, or you didn't stick to your budget. Either way, you must get on it immediately and find out the reason why this happened. It will take a little bit of trial and error, but in a couple of months, you must have each envelope categorized with exactly the right amount.

So, does it mean this is the end of the exercise? Well, creating money envelopes for your expenses is only one step of the process. Following this exercise doesn't mean that your finances are in order and you have financial freedom. It is merely a means of getting started and not the end of the journey. You can now do a deep dive and see where you can save. Even if you set aside a small sum, which you don't use or spend, and instead divert it to your emergency fund or let it, sit in your savings account, then you can collect it over period and use it to pay off any debts. Collect funds and use them to pay off any significant debts.

## Save More

### *Small saving goals*

Along with your budgeting and spending habits, another thing you must do is establish certain small savings goals. It can easily be achieved by making the smallest of contributions without sacrificing any of your necessary expenses. It can be something as simple as collecting all the change you get in a day and storing it in a container. It is almost like maintaining a piggybank for adults. Whenever you go grocery shopping, you must not only concentrate on what you buy, but the quantity as well. Ask yourself if you need as much as you are buying or if you can make any concessions there. If you do this, and you end up saving some money, then you must store this away for safekeeping in your piggybank.

From your existing budget, start looking for things on offer or see if certain stores are offering discounts if you make any bulk purchases. If there are any clearance sales and something you need is being offered at a throwaway price, then that's a good deal! Saving a little here and there will enable you to collect a substantial sum over time. Why don't you try practicing this for six months and see the sum you manage to save?

The amount that you collect like this is not for the emergency fund as you have already budgeted that in your expenses. Instead, this amount is to be used to get rid of any debts or reduce the outstanding bills on your credit card. Doing this over time will have a cascading effect as less outstanding will mean less interest to be paid and eventually you will be able to pay your debt off completely. This is, however, a long-term exercise, and you need to continue saving any amount that you can patiently. If you find yourself not motivated enough to save some small change, the easy way to motivate yourself is to try and make it fun. You can perhaps enter into a challenge with your spouse or a friend to see who manages to save more over a month. Ensure that the reward you set for yourself is not money related. The reward you set for such challenges can be something as simple as doing the other person's chores for a day or two. The competitive spirit will help you save more and having the added luxury of someone else washing your car or vacuuming your house is certainly an added bonus.

## *Short term investments*

If you have now got into the habit of saving with a fixed target in mind, you can help speed things up by investing those funds. By placing the funds in short-term investments, you will not only be able to make a quick buck on the side (provided you choose your investment wisely), but it will also help you attain your savings goal. You will learn more about the different types of investments in the subsequent chapters.

## *Employers saving/retirement plans*

In this case, you need to be aware of your company's policies. Does your employer offer employer-sponsored retirement plans like 401k, 403B, or any other plans? You must contact the concerned executive or contact the human resource department in your organization and find out all you can about this. In most cases, your employer may offer to match a certain portion of your contribution. Now, you need to find out the maximum that your employer is going to contribute and match that amount. For instance, for every two dollars you contribute to your retirement fund, your employer will add two dollars too. It is essentially a freebie that you can use to fatten up your retirement fund.

Also, your employer can deposit these amounts even before the IRS can touch them. So, this has a two-way benefit- a qualified plan from your employer not only helps add funds to your savings by matching a portion but it also helps save a lot on taxes. Only once you withdraw this money will you liable for taxes, but chances are if you are sticking to your budget plan you will not have to make any withdrawals before your retirement. So, it is a win-win situation for you. Do not pass up on this opportunity to save.

## *24-hour rule*

You are not alone. Most Americans give in to impulse purchases, regardless of whether they are online purchases or something that caught your eye in a store. However, the more you spend impulsively and on unplanned purchases, the less you are likely to save. The solution to that problem is to enforce a 24-hour rule strictly. Well, it is quite simple. The moment you see something that will amount to an unplanned purchase, don't give into the impulse. Instead, give yourself 24-hours to see whether you still want it or not. After 24 hours, if you still feel that you need that item, then go ahead and purchase it. However, most of the time after contemplating for 24-hours you will realize that you can do without the new piece of clothing or the fancy new gadget. All this means that you will be able to stick to your budget and not burn a hole in your pocket with impulsive shopping.

## *Treat and save*

Until now, all the options were about cutting down on your expenses and saving more. Now, let's look at a way where you don't have to stop yourself from indulging a little bit every now and then. However, there is a catch here. After you follow your budgeting strategy you might feel like you deserve to treat yourself. You might want to pamper yourself or do something, which makes you happy, and you have the funds to indulge your fancy now. Well, you can give in and indulge yourself, but there is a catch. You must save a sum equivalent to the amount that you decide to spend. Like I said, there's always a catch. This rule, when properly applied, creates a win-win situation where you don't feel like you are depriving yourself of something and at the same time, you manage to save. So, you are essentially spending and saving at the same time!

## *Cost in value of hours worked*

The other way to put a curb on unplanned or planned purchases which are more likely wants rather than needs is to convert the amount required into the hours you must work to earn the necessary funds. So, if you suddenly like a new pair of shoes, convert the value of those shoes into the number of hours you will need to work to pay off the cost of those shoes. For instance, if you need to work for 10 additional hours to purchase those shoes you want, it will certainly put things into perspective. The thought of extra work might change your mind about whether you want to purchase something or not. Try this method with all your non-budgeted expenses and see the new perspective you get on spending.

## Credit Card

If used correctly, it is a very useful thing to have, but the very same convenience also makes it the most terrible thing to have in certain cases. We will now discuss in detail all that can go wrong with a credit card and how to handle such issues.

Once you have a credit card, you are assigned a limit for the same. Knowing that you have an available spending limit puts you at ease. You probably don't think twice before you pull your card out and swipe to make a purchase. Now, at the end of the month, if you pay it off in full then it is okay. However, if you have made a minimum required payment, that is the first step into a vicious cycle of debt accumulation. Credit card companies charge huge interest on any rollover amount that is on the card, and it continues until you pay off the entire sum due.

Most people do not even bother to look at their statements properly and they see what the minimum due is, pay it and are content with this until the next time they feel like using the card and adding more roll-over balance on the card, thereby leading to more interest. This may feel okay to some people as it is an additional source for them to spend with other than their income, but eventually, you will reach a stage where the card limit is maxed out, and that is when the real trouble starts.

Now you do not have additional spending power but are stuck with a huge liability where depending on your card limit the huge amount of interest is being added every month without you spending a single cent on it, it puts tremendous pressure on your actual source of income to meet the minimum due required.

Once you have reached this situation, you have already dug a financial hole for yourself, and it is going to keep getting deeper unless to plan your way out of the debt. Also, at this stage, if your income does not let you make the minimum amount due required, then it is even worse. Not only will you be charged interest but there will be late fees and if the combination exceeds your card limit, over-limit fees as well. So essentially, having a credit card may seem like a good idea, but if not used wisely, you can get caught in a huge debt burden. Also to avoid collection calls, you will then be forced to resort to other types of debt to pay the minimum and keep your card current, like cash advances, balance transfers (getting an additional credit card) payday loans, etc. and what this does is dig the financial hole deeper and deeper.

Now what if you already are in this situation? Let's list down a few steps to get you out of that debt.

Firstly, you need to make a list of how many credit cards you have and what monthly amounts are due on each of them. Next you need to look at the interest rates of each card. Yes, different card companies have different interest rates. Then you need to choose the card with the highest interest rate and start making not just minimum payments but some additional amounts to help ease the burden. It's important to start getting the balance down. It can be a small amount to start with, but you have to start somewhere. Otherwise, there is no way you are going to get out of this mess unless you are willing to put in the effort to clear the debt. So, the first thing you need to do if you have any other existing credit cards with an available limit on them is to stop using them with immediate effect. Otherwise you are just going to make your problems worse. The best way to stop using the credit card if you are not disciplined enough to trust yourself is to cut them up. It may sound harsh giving up your only available line of credit, but what you need to realize is you are not just postponing the inevitable but also making the situation worse with additional debt. So rather than being in a deeper hole a couple of months down the line, you are taking away that option and disciplining your spending.

## *Eliminating your credit card debt*

Acknowledging that you are in a financial mess is the first step toward resolving it. You have to make a workable plan and stick to it even if you do not see results immediately. Be patient, and eventually you will see the results.

Now that you have decided to get rid of your credit card debt, how do you go about it? The obvious thing is to cut down and start saving, but that alone is not necessarily going to help you. So, you must first see how bad your situation is and whether you can manage it by cutting down on a few luxuries. If being a little frugal works, then that's great. If it doesn't, then sit down with a pen and paper and list down all the cards that you have and the current outstanding balance on each of them. See which one has the highest interest. Though it may sound like just juggling your outstanding balances from one card to another, see if there is a card with any limit available and which gives you an option of balance transfer. The reason for a balance transfer is that companies want you to have your outstanding debt with them so they can charge interest and make money. To do that, they give you attractive offers like transfer of your balance from another card onto this particular card. They will probably charge zero interest for a period of 60 days and, in some cases, even longer periods. If you use this option wisely and with discipline, it can be your first step toward reducing credit card debt.

Let's say you do have this option available to you. You need to transfer the outstanding balance of the card with the highest interest to another card, preferably with lower interest. However, at this point, it does not matter because of the limited choices available to you. Once done, this card is essentially paid off and for the other card, you will need to continue the minimum payment you were already paying before the balance transfer. If you do this, nothing changes and after the free period, you are back to repaying your debts. However, what you need to do is utilize the interest-free period with a vengeance and try to save as much as possible and put it all on this card. You will not be able to pay off the complete balance but what you will manage to do is knock off a big chunk of the sum payable with significant interest piled on top. You can repeat this exercise until you pay off your outstanding amount. However, if the amount is just too big and you see that this option is not going to solve your problem, then you need to look at alternatives. You may even find that you can do this transfer at a time when you have overtime or extra income. That works in your favor because when you pay off more than is due on the new credit card balance, at zero percent, you effectively drop the amount that you owe to a manageable level.

Before we look at the alternatives, there is another approach to this, and that is to take the card with the lowest outstanding amount and aim toward getting rid of that balance first. You must do this regardless of which card is charging the most interest. The reason for this is, although you may end up paying more money on interest trying to clear the outstanding balance on a card, it will give you the confidence to keep going. Apart from this, it will also help improve your credit rating, which in turn will open up options for you to resolve your debt issues. This is called the "snowball" effect and as you clear one small debt, you move onto the next smallest debt, so as to eliminate these.

Perhaps you have gone through your card statements and concluded that balance transfer is not going to be an option. You do not have any limit to play around with, and your credit is so low that you cannot apply for a new card to work with a balance transfer option. In such a case, you will need to seek some professional help and work with a credit-counseling agency, preferably one that is a non-profit organization. You can also borrow money from your retirement account like a 401k, borrow against your car or house, or explain the situation to a family member explaining the seriousness of your intentions to resolve your credit issues and take a loan from them.

## Debt Consolidation

You need to try debt consolidation when you have tried every other method to try and resolve your debts but are unable to do so. With your credit cards maxed out, chances are your credit score will also have been affected. Getting further credit in the form of new credit cards or loans will not be that easy. In such cases, you must try and pick the best lenders who offer the best rates for debt consolidation. This way, you can relieve yourself of the stress and worry of making multiple payments and will only have to worry about making one set payment. It will also help you potentially save hundreds if not thousands of dollars in interest.

Debt consolidation agencies offer different services and some of them have attractive offers like less interest chargeable or no prepayment fees. However, all this depends on how good your current credit score is. So, after researching, choose the one that suits your profile the best. If it looks like your situation is beyond repair where you have not only maxed out your cards but have missed payments too and your credit score has almost hit rock bottom, you may then want to consider Debt consolidation through a DCA or Debt Consolidation Agency. Be sure that the payments that are expected each month suit your income so that you can meet them easily.

## *Debt Consolidation Agency*

Now that it is well established that you alone cannot handle your debts, it is time to take a little professional help. Just because you have maxed out your credit cards and your credit score are low does not mean there are no alternatives. There are still a few options you can try. There are specific debt consolidation agencies that, in spite of a low credit score, are willing to give you a loan to pay off all your debts, and then you have to make a single payment to them every month. Though this option might turn out to be slightly costly initially, it is all that you are left with. Right now, you are left with very few other choices, so go ahead and take what you can and work out a plan that allows you to have a little left over after paying the loan and after accounting for your budgeted costs. This may be a slow, painful process, but it starts to get you working in the right direction. This should make life easier, because you no longer have creditors hounding you. The other advantage is that you only have to make one single payment which is easy to track and if you have created a program with your DCA that suits your current financial situation, you can start chipping away at this loan by adding that additional cost as a part of your budget.

Now let's say you don't qualify for a loan from a DCA either. This means that you are in a bad spot and that's before you even begin budgeting your expenses. You need to find a way to get from one day to another, in a situation this grim. Below are some options, which may work if you have not thought of them already.

## *DSA- Debt Settlement Agency*

The main reason you must choose a DSA is that once you have registered with one, they handle all the negotiations of your debt on your behalf with the creditors in an effort to try and settle the debt at less than the due amount. No collection agency can call you in regard to debt once you are registered with a DSA. That in itself will ease a tremendous pressure leaving you free to try and earn more. The way this works is the DSA will now call up your creditors on your behalf to try and settle your accounts for a value less than the current amount outstanding. What you need to note is this is applicable only if you have been defaulting on your loans and have not made payments for a few months on your cards. This option will further harm your credit, but right now, this will be a good way of getting out of debt and then learning from your past financial mistakes to make a fresh start with your budget.

## Refinance Your House

This is an option which is the most convenient but also the one which most people don't realize that they have. Yes, you have a mortgage on your house, and yes it has not yet been paid off, but what people don't realize is that property prices tend to appreciate over time and you may be eligible to get a refinance loan for the difference between the amount outstanding on the house and the value of the house. Also, with refinance the amount can be high and interest low, allowing you to either pay off all your debts and start afresh on your budget or at least pay some and settle some depending on your situation. Either way, your situation improves. It is important to realize that if you do not make payments on time for the remortgage, you could lose your home, so make sure that you do not take on more than you can easily afford to pay.

## Loan against Your Vehicle

If you do not have a mortgage or enough equity to refinance, you can see if there is an option to take a loan against your vehicle. There are many banks and credit unions you can approach to do this. Any additional money will help you get back on track for some time at least and give you a chance to change your financial situation and start adhering to your budget.

## Save on your Utility Costs

Another form of saving that many generally tend to overlook is saving on utility bills, and it does not even take that much of an effort to do this. Now that you have created a budget, you are already aware of exactly how much you have been spending on utilities. Try the following steps, and any money that gets saved gets apportioned to the most required section of your budget, whether it is your retirement fund or your emergency fund, etc. you will have prioritized the requirements by now.

- Reduce the temperature
- Try a ceiling fan
- Use windscreens to eliminate dust
- Replace your filters
- Try alternate methods of cooking
- Buy energy efficient appliances
- Make your home leak proof
- See if you can use solar.
- Reduce the temperature

It does not take a rocket scientist to figure this one out, yet most choose to ignore this obvious solution. Once the thermostat is set, no one thinks about changing it. However, if you reduce the temperature when you are stepping out of your house or when you are nice and cozy under your blankets, you can start saving. It has been estimated that for every eight hours of reduced temperature, as low as one degree, this can help lower your electricity bill by one percent.

If you are in a climate that does not require heating but just the opposite, don't immediately reach for the air conditioner. You can install some ceiling fans. Though installing the fans does not reduce the actual temperature, it does provide relief from the heat by circulating the air in your room. If this does not help, you can try a combination of AC and ceiling fan to help you out. Any small saving will eventually add up.

You can start using windscreens. The main reason for this is not to keep your windows open to let the air in and cool your house, but dust hampers the function of your appliances as well. When you are stocking your refrigerator, once in a while check to see if the coils below are blanketed in dust. These need to be cleaned regularly as a dust-covered coil needs to put in that much more effort, thereby leading to that much more electrical consumption.

Similarly, you must check the filters on your AC unit regularly. These trap the fine dust particles from the air before going onto the blower, giving you clean, cool air. However, as the dust becomes too much, it becomes an effort for the AC to pull in the air as the access is completely blocked by dirt, this puts additional load on your AC. The result, as you must have guessed by now, leads to higher electrical consumption.

By following these simple steps, you can significantly reduce your utility bills.

# CHAPTER THREE

# BECOMING A MINIMALIST

## Benefits of Minimalism

Minimalism is all about reducing clutter in your life so that you can start focusing on things that do matter. It is not just about eliminating physical objects, but is about decluttering your life mentally, physically, emotionally and even financially. Once you embrace this lifestyle, you can shift all your focus toward things that do matter. When you do this, you will be able to see all the opportunities that come your way. By opting for a minimalistic lifestyle, you don't have to stop spending money. Instead, you will learn to spend money only on the things that you need in life. All this will help maximize the benefits. In this section, you will learn about the different benefits minimalism offers.

### *Prioritizing your spending*

Minimalism allows and encourages you to embrace all the essential things. This habit will naturally translate into the way you spend and how much you spend. If you are not keen on acquiring materialistic possessions, then you will start to concentrate on experiences. This will change the way you spend your money. By understanding what matters the most to you, you can change your spending priorities, and only concentrate on what you need. All this helps increase your savings while making you more conscious of your spending habits.

## *Reduces your need for things*

When you embrace a minimalist lifestyle, you start to limit your need for things. Since you buy fewer items or own less, it is an effective means to decrease your spending and increase your savings. It can also mean that it becomes easier to clear your debts and attain the financial freedom you desire. If your purchases decrease, you can easily divert those funds to your savings and investment. It helps you focus on attaining your financial goals without making you feel like you are depriving yourself of anything.

## *You will need less*

By embracing minimalism, your need for storage space decreases. As you start prioritizing your belongings and only hold onto the things you need instead of all the clutter you have gathered over the years, you will need less room. When you declutter, you will realize you don't need a lot of physical space to live in. This, in turn, helps to cut back on the mortgage or rent you pay for a huge house. I don't mean that you need to shift to a smaller house, but that you always have an option of shifting to a smaller house. It is not only cost effective but will enable you to concentrate on things that matter.

## *Helps focus*

Minimalism and mindfulness go hand in hand. Mindfulness is an added benefit of minimalism. It is a quality that comes in handy while budgeting and creating your financial goals. Budgeting is all about spending according to a plan based on your current priorities. Once you understand what matters the most to you, it becomes easier to decide how much and when you spend your funds. It also helps you notice all those areas in life where you need to change your spending habits. By changing your spending habits and increasing your savings, you can easily attain financial freedom.

## *Clear your debts*

A simple way to get your finances in order is to clear all your debts. A lot of people start to clear off their consumer debts when they adopt a minimalistic lifestyle. As you get rid of debts, it stabilizes your finances and gives you some flexibility. Also, by reducing your debts, you can breathe a sigh of relief. You can use all the funds you are left with to do something you are passionate about. For instance, if you don't have any credit card bills to pay, you can use those funds to increase your savings or investments. Also, when you are aware of all your expenses, you can make provisions for these and cut back on your credit card use.

## *Sell what you don't need*

If you are just getting started with minimalism, then the best way to declutter is by selling everything that you don't need. You can use the funds from the sales proceeds to free up any clutter in your financial life. Maybe you can use the funds to pay off any small debts, start an emergency fund, or even use it for going on a trip you have always wanted to! As you start decluttering your life, you get a chance to fix any financial mistakes you made in the past. Organizing a garage sale is a rather simple way to get rid of all the clutter and make a quick buck on the side.

## *Simplification of your finances*

There are different things you can do to get a handle on your finances. You can start paying your bills on a single day or start using cash for your daily purchases. By doing this, it becomes easier to keep track of your expenses as well as how much you spend. You can also start using different online apps or expense tracking tools to help with the budgeting process. It helps ensure that you are sticking to your goals and aren't overspending.

## *Giving becomes easier*

When you are aware of all that which matters to you and have a hold on your finances, it becomes rather easy to give. Giving can be in terms of time or even monetary help. When you embrace minimalism, it becomes quite easy to see what and how much you can give without putting yourself in a tight spot. A simple change in your mindset and attitude toward finances can help attain your financial goals.

## Become a Financial Minimalist

A lot of people actually feel that their finances control them instead of it being the other way around. After going through the previous section, I am sure you must be excited about embracing a minimalistic lifestyle. In this section, you will learn about various practical tips you can use to become a financial minimalist.

### *Consolidating your bank accounts*

You can get by fine by just maintaining one savings account and a checking account. If you happen to have more accounts, then it is a good idea to consolidate all your accounts into one savings and one checking account. It helps simplify all the banking process you undertake without losing out on anything. This stands true for your retirement accounts too. If you have multiple accounts because of any previous employment you held with various 401k plans, then you merely need to consolidate them all into one self-directed IRA account. This reduces all the paperwork you need to do and also makes it easier to get an accurate picture of your total savings.

### *Reduce your paperwork*

As mentioned earlier, if you have multiple accounts for different financial investments, it means your paperwork will start to pile up. It can get to a stage where you no longer have the time to go through it all. Not just that, having a lot of paperwork to tackle merely increases your stress. By getting rid of all unnecessary paperwork and keeping only that which is a necessity, this will save you time and effort. In this modern world, you can check most of your transactions and statements online. If you are consolidating your accounts, then your paperwork will naturally reduce. Try to opt for all online banking services instead of the manual offline ones.

## Number of credit cards

A lot of people tend to have multiple credit cards. These shiny plastic cards are like a Pandora's Box. If you lose track of your finances, you can get in way over your head and might not even realize how far in debt you are. Having a lot of credit card debt can effectively ruin your credit score too. By maintaining only one credit card, you will become aware of your expenses and your dues too. Not just that, it is a great way to declutter your financial life. You must opt for a credit card that offers the best benefits and let go of all the rest.

## No debts

Debt not only costs you money, but it does make your life quite complicated. If your debts are too high, then your finances will start to control your life. This is certainly not a good way to live. Not only will you be spending all your time trying to pay your bills, but it also increases your debt. It is quite easy to lose control over your debts if you aren't careful. Apart from this, if most of your income goes toward the repayment of the debt, you will not be left with much, and it can make you feel overwhelmed. So, by eliminating your debts, you can make your life a little less complicated. One of the best ways to adopt a minimalistic life when it comes to finances is by becoming debt free. This isn't an overnight process and will take some time. However, if you focus on your goals and stick to your plan of action, you can be debt free.

## *Investing*

It is certainly more exciting and rewarding to invest in individual stocks instead of funds. However, it can get quite messy. You must do the necessary research, buy the stock, actively track its progress, and then sell it at the right time. You must do these things for every stock you own. If you own a couple of dozens of stocks, it can quickly become a fulltime job, even if you aren't interested in it. You can do away with all this hassle by selecting to invest in mutual funds. Funds are not only easier to manage, but it is quite easy to stay on top of all the tax requirements.

## *Reduce your expenses*

The best way to adopt a minimalistic attitude toward your finances is by reducing your expenses. To do this, you must first become aware of all your expenses. Go through the information given in the previous chapters to make a list of your expenses. A simple way to reduce your expenses is only to purchase those things that you need rather than things you want. If there is something that you feel like buying right now, wait for a month and see how you feel about it then. If you still feel like buying it, then you can. However, most of us tend to be impulsive shoppers, and by keeping your impulses in check, you can easily break free of consumerism.

Instead of eating out every day, you can start eating at home. Cooking your meals at home is a great way to reduce your expenses. Not just that, it also helps ensure that you eat healthy meals. If you are used to spending $5 every morning on a cup of coffee, you can start brewing coffee at home. If you spend $5 per day, that amounts to about $1800 per year! That's a lot of money you can save if you make coffee at home instead. You can start using public transport and walk short distances whenever feasible. You can also start eating common meals. A simple tip is to establish a weekly grocery and expenses budget for yourself and stick to it.

## *Paying cash*

It might sound rather old fashioned, given that going cashless seems to be the latest trend. Well, paying for your expenses with cash is a great way to become mindful of your expenses. When you pay with cash, then it becomes easier to keep track of your funds and expenses. When you go cashless, it is quite easy to lose track of your spending until your bills arrive. Whenever you make purchases using cash, you merely need to make your purchase and that's that. You don't have to worry about dealing with any payments to be made later or going through any bank statements. Also, it becomes easier to allocate a budget for your spending and stick to it. Only use your credit card when it becomes crucial and for any significant transactions.

## *No unnecessary services*

Most of us tend to have a lot of subscriptions we pay for monthly for services seldom used. If you are paying for a gym membership that you never use, then it is time to either end that subscription or start using it. If you have subscribed to multiple online streaming services like Netflix, then hold onto the one you like the most, and do away with the rest. By eliminating such unnecessary expenses, you can start saving a little. Also, fewer subscriptions mean you must make less payments, and this is an easy way to manage your finances.

## *Restrict your goals*

It is quite essential to establish specific goals and work toward achieving them. However, you cannot be successful if you set more goals than are practically attainable. It is critical that you set one - or at the most two - critical goals. Anything more than this and you will lose track of what needs to be done. Your concentration is like a bucket full of water. Every distraction is like a small hole in this bucket. If there are too many things you need to concentrate on, then there will not be any water left in the bucket. Setting too many goals is an easy way to lose focus on what is essential in life. Multiple goals tend to spread out your fixed assets like time, resources, and energy. Not just that, but it will also cause unnecessary confusion. To avoid all this, you must set a goal, attain it, and then move onto the next goal.

## *Increase your income-generating activities*

This tip usually applies to all those who are self-employed like freelancers. If you hold a 9-5 job, then you will have a fixed source of income. However, if you want to increase your productivity, then you must start concentrating on all those tasks that directly contribute to your monthly income. When you make a list of such tasks and jobs, it becomes easier to do away with the unnecessary tasks that don't contribute to your bottom line in any manner.

## *Too much information*

Information is essential to make informed decisions. However, too much information can be a bad thing since it causes a lot of needless confusion. Too much noise only increases mental clutter. You need to know when to stop. Everyone will have different opinions and different self-proclaimed "financial gurus" will give you various advice, which might not be suitable in your given situation. So, if you find something that works for you and you have a good feeling about it, stick to it. Don't overwhelm yourself with unnecessary information.

# CHAPTER FOUR

# WHEN MUST I INVEST?

## Should I invest if I Have Student Loan?

Well, it is a common belief that it is a good idea to pay off your debts before you think about investing. This becomes rather tricky, especially when you have significant debts like a student loan. You might think that you must first pay off your student loans once you start working and only then invest. However, is this the best way to go about doing things? Do you need to wait until you are debt free before investing? Or can you invest even when you have student loans? You will learn the answers to all these questions in this section.

When it comes to personal finance, there isn't one solution that can fit everyone's needs. You must analyze your current situation and then decide the best course of action. You must consider important factors like tax deductions, expected rates of return on investment, and the risks involved. Here are a couple of factors you must keep in mind while you debate about whether you must repay your student loans or invest.

## *Compound interest*

Interest doesn't have to be a bad thing necessarily. Most of us think it is terrible because interest starts kicking in on the student loan payments as soon as you start working. For instance, when you graduate with student debt or when you start using your credit card, a portion of the payments made is for the interest due on it every month. This can hinder your ability to repay your debt quickly and can end up increasing the duration of the loan. However, interest can be your ally when you earn it.

This is precisely what investing is about. You will essentially be making your money work for you and derive the benefits it offers. After a while, the interest on your investments tends to add up, and you will be pleasantly surprised with the sum you have earned. To do this, you must first consider if you can get a better return through investing than what you will save by paying off your student debt.

Depending on when the loan was taken along with the type of loan, the interest rates can be between 4 to 8%. Repaying your debt is as good as seeing a guaranteed return. For instance, the sooner you pay off a 5% student debt, then sooner you can start saving. However, what if an investment offers you a 7 to 8% interest? When you make a long-term investment with a reasonable rate of interest, then it will make it worthwhile to invest while paying off your student loans.

## *Tax deductions*

Another point you must consider are the tax benefits you can claim if you invest while repaying your student loans. According to your eligibility, you will be qualified to make a deduction of up to $2500 on your taxable income. Over time, this will make the interest payable on your loans less expensive. When it comes to numbers, the option of repaying your student loans or investing can be easily made by comparing your interest rate after taxes.

You can estimate your interest rate after taxes by using this simple formula:

Student loan interest rate X (1-marginal tax rate).

If the interest payable on your student loan is 5% while filing income tax as a single individual, and your income is $50,000 a year, then it places you in the 22% bracket for 2019. By using the formula mentioned above, you will get an interest rate of

3.9%. So, essentially, the interest rate payable on your student loans is about 3.9%.

So, if you manage to get an annual return of about 7% on your investments, then you can easily make up for the 3.9% interest payable toward the student loan. If the numbers work out favorably, then it is a good idea to invest while only making the minimum repayments on your student debt.

## *List your priorities*

Not everything is related to numbers, and you must also consider your priorities while thinking about repaying your student loans or investing. Some essential goals you might need to include the following.

You might need to consider saving up for any emergencies. It is quintessential that you create an emergency fund. You need to save up at least a couple of thousand dollars as an emergency fund before you think about working toward any other goals. If you have any high-interest debts, then it is a good idea to clear those dues before anything else. For instance, if you have a credit card debt at 17.99% interest, then repaying it is a wise choice. Apart from this, you must also consider how much you want to start saving for your retirement. Creating a nest egg is essential to secure your future. You might also have some significant life plans like getting married, buying a house, or even starting a family. Make a list of all your priorities along with the funds they require. Once you do this, you can get a read on your financial situation. You can then consider whether you need to repay your student debt before investing or not.

## Is 401k Sufficient for Retirement?

A 401k plan enables employees to make certain deductions from their salary as a contribution toward their retirement fund. Most of the 401k plan deductions are made before taxation, but this differs from one employee to another. Your employer can either match your contribution to the 401k plan or even offer to make a non-elective contribution. The earnings or contribution toward the 401k are on a tax-deferred basis.

Usually, there are specific caps placed on the contributions, which can be made to the 401k. The Internal Revenue Service or IRS has specific regulations in place that limit the percentage of salary that can be a 401k contribution. In 2019, the cap on 401k contribution is set at $19,000, and it is $500 more than the previous year's limit. For an individual making $150,000 per year, the 401k contribution gives them a savings rate of about 12.7%. If your income exceeds $150,000, then the savings rate tends to reduce. Having a savings rate of about 12% is certainly not ideal to meet your requirements post-retirement.

The cap on contributions to a 401k for the year 2019 is $56,000 from any source, and for those over the age of 50 years, they can add the contribution of about $6000 as a catch-up contribution. All contributions to the 401k need to be made before 31st December.

So, a 401k plan might not be sufficient for your retirement, and here are the reasons.

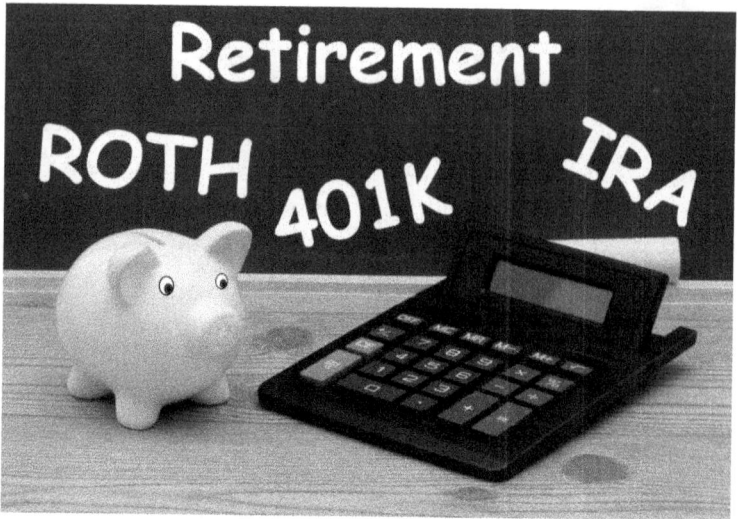

### *Taxes and inflation*

The cost of living is never constant, and it has been increasing steadily. A common mistake made while calculating the retirement requirement is that a lot of people overlook the effect of inflation. Retirees tend to think that they have plenty of funds in their retirement funds or 401ks. They think that they have financial freedom and then the hard reality hits them. The cost of living increases while their funds stay the same. Even if it might sound like you have sufficient funds at the moment, this requirement will change because of inflation.

Apart from this, there is the problem of taxes that you must not overlook. An advantage offered by 401k is that it is tax deferred. It essentially means that the 401k will grow without accrual of taxes. However, once a retiree starts to make withdrawals from the 401k, the same will be added to their yearly income, and it will attract income tax at the current rates at that time. This rate, just like inflation, will probably be higher than what was assumed by the retiree 20 years ago. The 401k created by an individual during their 20s or 30s might not turn out to be as bountiful as they might have hoped.

All the money in the 401k is tax deferred. It means that for every dollar you save now, it will only amount to be about 65 to 80 cents depending on your tax bracket. So, if you save a million dollars, it will not necessarily mean that you have a million dollars to spend after retirement. You need to save in the 401k with a margin of at least 30% if you want to maintain the lifestyle as you do now.

## *Other fees and costs*

The fees and other costs associated with the 401k can be quite steep at times. These costs can affect your bottom line and even reduce your savings. There are several fees that are left undisclosed, like bookkeeping fees, legal fees, finder's fees, and trustee fees. This can easily overwhelm you, and if you aren't careful, you can get fleeced. This is apart from any other fund fees payable. Mutual funds included in 401k tend to charge an outright fee of 2%. If a fund gives you a 7% interest but then charges you a fee of 2%, you aren't left with the kind of returns you will have expected. So, if you aren't careful, it can run into thousands of dollars that you will lose out on. If you want to save, then you need to take into account all the charges payable while calculating the savings you are making.

### *Lack of liquidity*

Mostly all the funds that you put in the 401k account are safely locked away, and they cannot be fully accessed until the individual reaches a certain age or when they have an excellent reason to incur the penalties on an early withdrawal. Unlike other forms of investment, a 401k account doesn't offer any liquidity. You must not think of your 401k as an emergency fund or an account you can dip into to finance a major purchase. If you ever need to make an early withdrawal from this account, the charges you incur are rather expensive. If you make a withdrawal before you are fifty-nine and a half years, then you will be attracting a 10% penalty. All the withdrawals are taxable, and the amount of tax payable will depend on the income bracket you fall under. The higher the tax bracket; the higher the taxes will be that you need to pay. It is not possible to invest or even spend money for cushioning your life without incurring a significant financial expenditure. However, borrowing from the 401k is an exception to this rule. You can certainly borrow money from your 401k, but it is a short-term loan. Also, you need to repay it within a fixed period and the period given in usually sixty days.

So, what's the bottom line? A 401k will certainly help accumulate funds for your retirement, but it might not be sufficient. As prudence suggests, it is a good idea to make other investments to make sure that you have a comfortable investment. You must never place all your eggs in one basket, and by having a diversified portfolio of investments, you can ensure that you have the financial freedom you desire even in your retirement.

## Setting up an Emergency Fund

Building an emergency fund not only takes time, but it requires dedication too. An essential part of becoming debt free is setting up an emergency fund. A lot of people have different opinions about how to go about doing this. For instance, it is a general belief that your emergency fund must have three to six months of your earnings as savings. As long as you only think of it as a general rule of thumb, it is fine. However, it can take people a couple of years to attain this goal. Also, while saving for this, how can they manage all their other expenses? Is it sufficient to only save three to six months' worth of income?

### *How much must you save for emergencies?*

According to the famous finance guru, Dave Ramsey, it is better to start with $1000 and then tackle your debt. If your monthly expenses amount to $10,000, then by saving $1000, you can only cover an emergency that spans over three days. Well, this doesn't sound reassuring. Instead of searching for a magic number, you must consider different factors while deciding the amount you need to save for a rainy day. In this section, you will learn about the different factors you must consider, and they are as follows.

A financial catastrophe is something you cannot afford to ignore while setting up an emergency fund. If you have a mortgage on your apartment and then lose your job due to unforeseeable conditions, then it might mean moving back with your parents. Always prepare for the worst-case scenario while setting up an emergency fund.

You must consider the interest rates payable on any debts you have. For instance, if you have a significant credit card debt carrying an interest of over 18%, then the best thing you can do is start clearing up your dues as quickly as you possibly can. If the interest rate on your debt is comparatively low, then you can pace your repayments accordingly.

The amount that you need to set aside for an emergency fund will also depend on your access to cash if an emergency presents. If you cannot easily access a line of credit or get your hands on the funds you need in an emergency, then the amount you set aside for a rainy day needs to be rather substantial.

Nothing is guaranteed in life, and there will be circumstances that can easily catch you unawares. The risk of losing your job is a real possibility unless you have permanent employment. That is quite rare, and the risk of job loss is a possibility that you cannot afford to ignore. There is no fundamental rule that you can follow, and you need to analyze your situation while making any plans carefully. If you have good enough job security, then the amount that you set aside for an emergency fund doesn't have to be too large.

If you have several sources of income, then you can consider the option of paying off your debt while maintaining small savings. Your job stability, along with your source of income, can influence your emergency fund requirements. Apart from this, another thing you must consider is the 401k plan. Does your employer make matching contributions to it? Then this is an excellent way to start creating a fund for your retirement. However, as mentioned in the previous chapter, this must not be the sole source of retirement funds.

## *Steps to build an emergency fund*

Here are the different steps that you must follow while creating an emergency fund for yourself.

### Track your income and expenditure

The first thing you must do is start by saving an amount equivalent to the expenses you incur in a month. This amount must include any sum that goes toward investing or debt repayment. Once you save funds equivalent to one month's expenses, you need to split any extra money you are left with between repaying any debts and adding it to your emergency fund. If your employer matches your contribution to the 401k, then you must try to make the most of it and build it up on that. By doing this, you will be able to effectively save, invest, and even pay off any debts you have.

You need to start tracking all the expenses you incur in a month along with the income you earn. You can use an online tool or an app like Track Your Spending to do this. If you want, you can also make a note of the same in a journal. By making a note of your expenses and income, you will get an idea of how much you spend and the amount you can save. You must include all recurring expenses like insurance premiums, mortgage payment, utility bills, and even make provisions for expenses like childcare and any other expenses you can incur when you go out.

## Setting a goal

Your emergency fund must cover at least three to six months' worth of your expenses, i.e. the amount you set as a goal for your emergency fund. If you feel that you have a stable source of income or have access to any quick means of funds, then your emergency fund can be a slightly lower figure. You must set a goal. If not, the chances of procrastination setting in are quite high. Set a realistically attainable goal for your emergency account.

## Plan of action

Once you set a goal, you must develop a plan of action to attain that goal. You can include certain measurable and specific goals to work toward. For instance, you can set a goal of increasing your monthly contribution to the emergency fund by about $150 per month.

## Accessible

The emergency fund that you create needs to be easily accessible too. If you place your funds in a place where you cannot access them, it will become rather difficult in case of an emergency. For instance, if you save your funds in the form of a real estate investment, then the liquidity it offers isn't high. However, if you save your funds in the form of cash, you can readily access it as and when the need arises. Saving your funds in a savings account in a bank is a good idea. You will not only be earning interest on your funds, but it is a risk-free form of investment when compared to other options. You must ensure that your funds can be easily accessed when needed as if not, it defeats the purpose of creating an emergency fund. Even if you have tens of thousands of dollars saved away as an emergency fund, what good will it do if you cannot access them?

## Sticking to your plan

Once you create your plan, you must follow it. Allow provisions for a couple of deviations, but not too many. A tricky part of creating an emergency fund is that saving money isn't a simple task. If the goals that you set are attainable, then it becomes easier to follow your plan. An excellent way to do this is by automating the process of saving funds. You can set up an automatic system of transfer of specific sum form your savings account or checking account and get it transferred to another account for safekeeping. Also, please ensure that the funds you save for an emergency don't get mixed up with any other savings or investments you want to make.

Once you have attained your goal for creating an emergency fund, the next step is to use any extra cash you have towards repaying your debts, if you have any. You can use those extra funds for investing or even add them to your savings for retirement. Now that you are aware of the different steps that have been enumerated in this chapter along with the other factors, which you must consider while setting up an emergency fund, the next step is to start planning it all out.

# CHAPTER FIVE

# RISK-FREE INVESTMENT

You are free to invest in more than one type of instrument and you certainly don't have to restrict yourself. One way in which you can reduce volatility is by diversification of assets or investments. You can include a couple of alternative assets like commodities along with risk-free and low-risk investments to mitigate the risk of loss. By including commodities to your portfolio, you can easily counteract the effects of inflation on your investments. Well, even when the price of other investments like stocks or mutual funds decreases during inflation, the price of commodities tends to shoot up. If you aren't keen on taking any risks or have limited risk tolerance, then you must invest in an instrument when the market is stable. It is all about trying to earn a profit even when the market seems bearish or bullish. Even when the value of your investments, like real estate, antiques, and other valuables hasn't been updated in the quarterly brokerage statement, you must know the value of your investment portfolio. Even if such items aren't sold off easily, their value and associated risks needs to be taken into consideration before you consider expanding your portfolio.

There are a couple of things that you must never do while you are designing and assembling your investment portfolio. Most of the investors tend to make certain mistakes that you must avoid. You must ensure that your investment decision is not based on a market fad. Don't follow any random fads that crop up. Instead, your investment decisions must always be based on thorough research and understanding of the financial markets along with the instruments. You cannot have a "set it and forget it" mentality when it comes to investing. You must review your investment portfolio and make changes as needed. You must diversify and change your pattern of asset allocation to mitigate the risk on investment. It takes a long time to make up for any setback that your portfolio might have encountered. So, be thorough in your research before you decide about investing.

## Bank Savings

A savings account generates income on the deposits that you hold at the bank or any other financial institution. The interest rates offered aren't too high and are quite modest. Financial institutions often offer such savings account, which limits the number of withdrawals that can be made. They might also levy a certain fee unless a specific minimum balance is maintained in the account.

So, how does this work?

A savings account is usually opened to save such money that doesn't have any immediate or daily expenses. A savings account is quite different from a checking account. As the name suggests, a checking account makes provision for using checks along with any electronic means of debt for accessing the funds. Also, savings account tends to limit the number of withdrawals or the transactions to be made by the account holder every month, and this might not be necessarily applicable to a checking account.

How can a savings account help you?

The importance of maintaining a savings account cannot be overlooked. It helps you set some money aside for your financial needs. You can use this account to save funds you need for holidays, college tuitions, or even a wedding. Other expenses that you can pay for with your savings are purchasing any real estate or a car perhaps. However, there are other means to pay for these, and holding a savings account is merely one option available. In this section, you will learn about the different benefits of using a savings account as a means of investment.

A savings account is an interest-based account wherein interest gets accrued over a period. Please don't be under any misconceptions that opening a savings account is similar to maintaining a piggybank. When you place some money in the piggy bank, the funds neither increase nor decrease and stay the same. However, when you deposit money in a bank, then your account gets credited with a certain amount as interest every year. So, you can substantially increase your finances, while making sure that there are no risks involved. Opening a savings account is believed to be one of the safest methods of investment.

You can certainly reach for your credit card whenever you lack any money and might look for other means to fund your needs, instead of spending money that you didn't have and then worrying about increasing your debt. You must start controlling your use of credit cards. A credit card will not do you much good if you get stuck in a rather unfortunate situation. For instance, if you lose your job, how can you cover all your basic needs using a credit card? Surely you can make do until your credit limit is exhausted, but then again you will need to think about the repayment as well.

Another great thing about the modern banking system is that your funds are available and can be accessed at any point in time. You don't have to worry about time zones or boundaries.

However, on the downside, the rate of interest offered by banks on a savings account is quite low when compared to any other form of investment. Apart from this, there are several restrictions placed on the number of withdrawals you can make along with a minimum balance you must maintain.

## Zero Coupon Bonds

Zero coupon bonds are basic bonds that follow extremely simple rules. Here, there are no complications, and everything is straightforward. Now, say for example you buy bonds worth $400 today that have an expiry date five years from now. Once they reach their maturity period, these bonds will be worth $800 each. So, for a period of five years, you will receive a consistent rate of interest for your investment. These are extremely safe choices for you, and the rate of interest is also higher than what your federal government or agency will pay.

Here, the bond that you receive today will actually be worth $800. However, you will get it at a big discount now and then cash it in, in full, after a certain amount of time. Don't think of this as a bad scheme, as your money will be safe, and you will have the chance to double what you have in due course.

It is, however, not comparable to stocks, as it might not take so long to receive a return on your investment. Bonds are safer options for you, but you will not be able to invite large returns from these types of investments.

There are many situations where people can use zero coupon bonds. A basic example is a parent saving money for his or her child's college fund. It is easy to invest money that will mature by the time a child is college age. This will help pay for the cost of college. Another example is wealthy people using zero coupon bonds to leave as an inheritance for family members. These beneficiaries do not have to pay as much tax as they would if it was not a bond. Sometimes zero-coupon bonds are tax exempt, especially those issued by a government agency while those issued by a corporation are not tax exempt. For these kinds of bonds, you will have to pay income tax for earning that you have not yet received.

## Government Bonds

Government bonds are those that are issued by the government. This means that these bonds are securities that the government of your country will issue for you. Government bonds can be issued by both the central and the state government. These bonds are money that the government borrows from the public. The government needs this money to carry out their various businesses, including construction, renovation, repair, etc. Although the government will already have some money, it cannot operate on that money alone.

These types of bonds have existed for a long time, and the government has issued millions of bonds to date. That makes for a debt of nearly 20 trillion dollars owing to all the bonds that have been issued to date. Here, you must understand that the government will collect taxes from citizens and try to recover the money for the bonds. However, the amount collected will often be insufficient, and several bonds will have reached maturity date. Now, they cannot turn away the people that they have not paid as yet, and they must ensure that everybody gets their money. Under such a circumstance, they will borrow this money and pay off their bondholders. Doing this for a long time can cause the economy of a country to destabilize. This destabilization can affect those who invest in stocks, as people are not going to spend as much during an economic crisis, no matter how big or small it seems.

However, from an investor's point of view, this is a good investment as there is minimal credit risk at play. This means that there is no real danger of the investor not getting his or her money back in full. Thus, government bonds make for the right choice for all those looking for a safe option to invest in. However, you must remember that your credit risk needs to be high if you wish to make the most of your investment.

"High risk, high reward" is the ultimate anthem of the stock market, and with bonds, that is not a possibility. Although there will be the danger of you losing half or all your money in credit risk investments, the possibility of doubling or even tripling is high. This makes it a worthwhile investment for you because you don't have to worry about suffering any losses.

There are different types of government bonds that you can choose from. Each one comes with its own set of advantages, and you have to choose the one that suits your investment type the best. Many brokers these days will advise you against investing in these bonds, as the American debt level is consistently rising. However, the ultimate choice lies with you alone, and you will have to decide for yourself whether you want to invest in government bonds!

The type of bond you can buy from the government is dependent on the bond's maturity. Short-term bonds are called bills, and they mature in less than a year. Notes are the medium-term bonds that mature between one and ten years. While bonds themselves are the long-term ones, who take more than ten years to mature, these bonds are better known as treasury bonds or treasury bills.

## Certificate of Deposit

A certificate of deposit or a CD is essentially a savings certificate that has a fixed date of maturity along with a fixed interest payable to its holder. If you invest your funds in a CD, then your access to those funds is restricted until the instrument reaches its maturity. These instruments are usually issued by commercial banks and the Federal Deposit Insurance Corporation or FDIC insures them for up to the amount of $250,000 per investor.

A bank usually issues CDs that are promissory notes. It is a time-bound deposit, which restricts its holder from withdrawing the funds as and when they please. It is usually issued in electronic form and can also be automatically renewed upon its maturation. Whenever a CD matures, then the holder of the CD can withdraw the principal along with all the accrued interest. No additional fees are chargeable on a CD if they are withdrawn before they mature. The interest rates offered by most CDs happen to be higher than the one offered by savings accounts.

CDs are based on the idea that you can get a higher return by giving up liquidity for the time being. Under usual market conditions, the interest rates on long-term CDs is slightly higher than the ones offered on short-term CDs. The rate of return provided by CDs isn't exceptionally high and is certainly not more than the returns that you can get from stocks or other high-risk investments. The good thing about investing in CDs is that your funds are secured until their maturity. Not only are they secure, but you will also earn interest on them. If you make an early withdrawal from a CD, then you are liable to pay an early withdrawal penalty and this amount depend on the duration of the CD along with the institution issuing it. Early withdrawal penalties are usually equivalent to the interest payable.

CDs are usually non-negotiable. Simply put, it means that the instrument cannot be transferred, exchanged, or even sold.

Usually, a non-negotiable CD is eligible for an early withdrawal prior to its maturity provided you pay the early withdrawal fees. On the other hand, negotiable CDs or NCDs are the exact opposite of a non-negotiable CD. NCDs are usually issued for large denominations and tend to have a maturity period between a two-weeks until one year. Any CD issued for less than $100,000 is referred to as small CDs. At times, some CDs might also require a minimum investment. Usually, negotiable CDs can be either small or large CDs.

## Money Market Funds

Any type of mutual fund which primarily invests in instruments that with a high liquidity like cash, cash equivalents, or any other securities with a high credit rating with a short-term maturity are referred to as money market funds. The liquidity offered by these funds is quite high whereas the associated risks are almost negligible. Money market funds are also referred to as money market mutual funds and function like any other regular mutual fund. They are issued in the form of redeemable instruments or shares to the interested individuals and the must be in compliance with all the rules and regulations given by the United States Securities and Exchange Commission.

A money market fund can invest in any type of debt-backed financial instrument like certificates of deposits, commercial paper, banker's acceptance, treasury bills, as well as any other repurchase agreements.

## Investment in Dividend Shares

Most people tend to invest in dividend-based stocks to take advantage of the endless benefits they promise, as well as the reinvestment opportunities they offer to buy additional stock. The majority of the dividend-bearing shares are companies that are generally considered to be financially sustainable, and there is a possibility that dividends will increase steadily over some time. In the meantime, the shareholder may receive regular distributions in the form of dividends. For example, a company may receive a dividend of 205% for one year and increase it to 3% next year. However, this cannot be said with certainty. As soon as the company gains a reputation for reliable dividends that will increase over time, it will strive not to disappoint its investors.

A company that can pay steadily increasing dividends is financially stable and generates sufficient cash flow (as dividends are declared from revenues). Such companies are considered stable, and their share prices are not as volatile as other companies. Dividend-paying stocks are considered to be less risky and therefore more attractive to young investors looking for long-term returns as well as to retirees or retirees. This is a good source of income. The ratio between the stock price and the dividend yield also strengthens investor confidence. When share prices fall, earnings per share increase.

## Warrants

A warrant is similar to an option. The holder has the right and not an obligation for buying the underlying security at a specified price and quantity at some time in the future. An option is an instrument that is traded on the stock exchange, whereas a company will issue a warrant. The security that is represented by the warrant, usually an equity share, will be delivered by the company issuing it instead of the investor holding those shares. Companies usually include warrants as a part of their new issue offering. This is offered for attracting investors and also for improving the confidence of a shareholder in the stock. This is conditional to an actual increase in the value of the underlying security over a while. A warrant is a kind of equity derivative.

For instance, shares of a company have a market value of $1.50 per share. You will need to invest $1500 to purchase 1000 shares. However, if the investor opted to invest in warrants (where one warrant represents one share) that were priced at $.50 per warrant, then such an investor would be in the ultimate possession of 3000 shares for the same investment. The leverage and the gearing that is offered by warrants tends to be high due to their low price. This will mean that the potential for reaping capital gains will be more significant. It is quite common that the warrant and share price might be moving in a parallel fashion. However, the proportion of likely gain or loss will differ significantly due to the fundamental difference in their pricing. Another illustration will help you to gain a better understanding of this concept. For instance, the share of a company records a gain of $.30 per share from the initial price of $1.50, it will be $1.80. This shows a 20% gain. However, if the price of a warrant goes from $.30 to $.80, this will indicate a 60% hike. In the given situation, the gearing factor is arrived at by dividing the initial price of the share by the initial price of the warrant ($1.50/$.50 = 3). The gearing factor in this case is 3, and it shows the financial leverage offered by the warrant. The greater this number is, the higher is the potential for profits or losses.

When the market is bullish, the gains offered by warrants are quite significant. They also provide the investor with protection during a bearish market. As the price of the underlying shares drops, the warrants wouldn't probably realize the same loss as compared to the underlying shares. This financial leverage that's offered comes in quite handy.

The leverage that's offered by this instrument is often high. However, this can work to the investor's disadvantage as well. Let us take into consideration the example that was mentioned above. If you have realized a drop by $.30, then the percentage of loss on the share will be 20%, and that incurred on a warrant will be 60%. An increase is always favorable. However, a drop in the same price can prove to be a more considerable disadvantage. The next risk that the investor will face will be that the value of a warrant certificate can plummet to zero as well. If this happens before the rights were to be exercised, then the warrant wouldn't have any redemption value. A warrant doesn't carry any voting rights. The investor won't have a say in any matters regarding the functioning of the company, though their rights will be affected by the company's decision.

# CHAPTER SIX

# LOW-RISK INVESTMENT

## Corporate Bonds

When it comes to investments, you do not have to invest only in equities, but can also invest in debt instruments. You, as an investor, can choose the asset class that you want to invest in based on your risk tolerance. There are different categories of debt instruments. This section provides some information on one category of debt fund schemes known as corporate bond funds.

### *Corporate Bond Debt Funds*

A corporate bond debt fund or a non-convertible debenture can be issued by any company. Companies that want to expand their business or improve their daily operations can use these funds to raise capital for the company. Companies can choose to raise funds through debt or equity investments. Since debt does not affect a shareholder directly, most companies choose to invest in debt funds. It is for this reason that most companies go in for debt. A corporate bond debt fund gives a company an economic way to raise funds when compared to opting for a bank loan.

A corporate bond security is the foundation for any credit opportunity for a debt fund. When you purchase a debt fund, you are loaning the company some money. The firm will only repay the loan amount at the end of the term and will give you an interest amount every month. This interest amount is called the coupon.

## *Who must invest in a Corporate Bond?*

A corporate bond is a good investment choice for you if you are looking for a higher but fixed income from a safe investment option. This investment instrument is a low-risk investment vehicle, and it also ensures some capital protection. If you want to choose a corporate bond fund that puts your money in a high-quality fund, it will serve your financial goal.

A long-term debt fund is often risky since the interest rate will fluctuate beyond the expectations. A corporate bond will always invest in scraps, which will reduce the volatility of the bond. Most corporate bonds can only have a maturity date between one and four years. This is an added benefit if you choose to invest in the bond for more than three years. You can also use this investment to help you be more tax efficient.

## *Benefits and Features of a Corporate Bond*

## Components of a Corporate Bond

A corporate bond fund will always invest in a debt paper. Most companies issue a debt paper that includes debentures, bonds, structured obligations and commercial papers. The components listed in the debt paper will carry a maturity date and will also carry a unique risk profile.

## Price of the Bond

It is important to remember that no bond is static, and that it always has a price. The price of the bond will change depending on when you choose to purchase the bond. You must always see how the value of the bond varies from the par value, and this difference will explain the par value of the bond.

## Par Value of the Bond

The par value of the bond is the amount of money that the issuer of the bond, mostly the company, will give you when the bond matures. This is basically the principal amount. The par value of the bond is usually $100.

## Coupon

When you purchase a corporate bond, the company will pay you a regular interest until you sell the bond, or the bond matures. This interest amount is called the coupon amount and is calculated as a percentage of the par value.

## Current Yield

The current yield is defined as the annual return that you will make from the corporate bond. For instance, if you own a bond that has a par value of $100, and the rate of the bond is

20%, you will receive an interest of $20 every year from that bond.

## Yield to Maturity

The yield to maturity is the in-house rate of return that the company receives for every cash flow associated with the bond. You will receive higher returns when the yield to maturity is greater, and vice versa.

## Tax Efficiency

You will need to pay a capital gains tax if you choose to hold the corporate bond for a period less than three years. The amount of tax you will be paying is dependent on your income. If you choose to invest in a long-term investment, you will not have to pay a higher tax.

## Allocation and Exposure

Most corporate bond funds are exposed to a government security as well, but this is only done if there is no opportunity available to issue the bond in the credit space.

## *Risk Factors and Returns*

There is a possibility that a bond issuer will default on its obligations. If the company issuing the bond has a lower rate, the possibility of default is higher. Additionally, as the maturity increases, the risk also increases. The risk is minimal when it comes to those companies that have a higher rating. If your fund manager only invests in companies with a higher rating, you can only gain an average return between eight and ten percent.

That being said, it is a good idea to invest in a bond issued by a company that has a low rate. For example, a company with bonds that give a higher coupon rate will always attract more investors. There is also the chance that your call or your fund manager's call will go wrong. It is because of this that the corporate bond can be a setback for an investor if the company chooses to default on its interest payments or the rate of the company goes down further.

## How Do Corporate Bonds Make Returns?

A mutual fund is much like a fixed deposit, in the sense that it also invests in tradable bonds. Like the share market, there is also a debt market that allows you to trade with numerous bonds. The price of the bonds will fluctuate in this market in the same way that the prices of the shares fluctuate in the share market. For example, if any bond is purchased by a mutual fund, the price of that bond will increase. The bond can then make additional money. This money is more money when compared to the interest of the bond alone. This can also be the other way around.

## Types of Corporate Bonds

There are two types of corporate bonds that you can invest in.

### Type One

Only high-rated companies like banks and public sector units (PSU) can issue a type one corporate bond.

**Type Two**

Companies that are rated slightly lower, that is an AA rating or below, can issue type two corporate bonds.

Let us look at the following example to better understand this concept. Suppose, a company that is rated A has a bond that has a default percentage of 0.56% and a one-year residual maturity, while another company rated A has a bond that has a default percentage of 4.79% and a three-year residual maturity. Corporate Bond funds often use the bonds issued by the companies with AA rank or lower in most of their portfolios. It is for this reason that there is a risk that some of the bonds will default, which will result in an impact on the returns from the portfolio.

## *Points to Remember*

There are some points you must remember before you choose to invest in a corporate bond fund.

1. Every corporate bond fund will always invest in different corporate bonds or debentures of long or medium tenure. So, it is important that you look at this type of investment as a long-term investment vehicle.

2. It is important that you have some knowledge about the market in this instance. If you are not someone who has invested in debt funds before, you will find it difficult to understand the market and the risks.

3. You must always look at the past-year returns for a corporate bond before you invest in it. That being said, you must never let it sway you because a large number

of defaults within the profile will lead to a drag in the returns.

4.  You must always stick to large AMCs when you choose the corporate bond you want to invest in. Always make a list of the top five AMC funds, and only invest in those. If you do not invest in these, you must stick to another high-rated short-term debt fund where you have a lower credit risk.

# Preferred Stocks

A preferred stock, also known as a preference share or preferred share is a security that will represent the ownership that a shareholder has in a corporation. These shareholders will have a priority claim over some common shares in the company's assets and earnings. A preferred share has a higher priority when compared to an ordinary share but is not as important as a bond when compared to other assets. A shareholder with preference shares has a higher priority when compared to those who hold common shares or stocks.

## *Features of Preferred Shares*

A preferred share has many features that are a combination of both a common equity and debt. The terms of the investments may vary, but there are some common features:

### Preference in Assets upon Liquidation

A preferred share gives every shareholder more priority when compared to a common shareholder, especially when the company is about to be liquidated.

## Dividend Payments

Every share will give the shareholder a dividend payment, and the payments can either be floating or fixed. This is dependent on a rate benchmark that is provided by LIBOR.

## Preference in Dividends

Every preferred shareholder will have some priority over a common shareholder when it comes to the dividend payments.

## Non-Voting

Most shares do not give their shareholders their own voting rights. That being said, some of preference shareholders are given additional rights when it comes to their votes.

## Convertibility to Common Stock

You can convert a preferred share into a common share depending on the agreement. There are some preference shares that will specify the dates on which these shares need to be converted. That being said, there are some shares for which there must be an approval provided by the board of directors.

## Callability

Every share can be repurchased by the issuer on some dates depending on what is agreed upon between the issuer and the shareholder.

## *Types of Preferred Stocks*

Preferred stocks are the perfect type of investment that you as an investor can make. There are different types of preferred stocks.

### Convertible Preferred Stock

A convertible preferred share can always be converted into an ordinary share. The management can determine the number of ordinary or common shares the investor can convert the preferred stock into.

### Cumulative Preferred Stock

If the issuer does not pay the dividend on the said date, the amount will be added to the next payment.

### Exchangeable Preferred Stock

The investor can choose to exchange a preferred share for any other type of security.

### Perpetual Preferred Stock

There is no guarantee when the shareholder can receive the capital.

## *Advantages of Preferred Shares*

Both the holders and the issuers of a preferred share will benefit from it. An issuer may be benefitted in the following ways through preferred shares:

## No Dilution of Control

This type of financing will allow an issuer to either defer or avoid the dilution of control, as the shareholders do not have the right to vote when they own these instruments.

## No Obligation for Dividends

The issuer of the share is not obligated to pay any dividend to the shareholder. This means that the company can choose to avoid paying a dividend if it does not have the necessary funds to make the payment.

## Flexibility of Terms

The terms for any preferred share can be discussed and agreed upon by the management or board of the company.

A preferred share is an attractive alternative investment for most investors. You as an investor can be benefited in the following ways:

## A Secure Position in Case the Company Is Liquidated

Every investor who has a preferred share is always in a better condition when compared to an investor who only owns common shares. These shareholders have a priority in claiming the assets of the company.

## Fixed Income

Most companies can and are willing to pay their shareholders a dividend every year. They are always willing to pay the shareholder a fixed income.

# Annuities

An annuity is a great investment to consider if you wish to earn a steady income during your retirement. You must understand what the different types of annuities are and how they work. This chapter will shed some light on different annuities. You must use this information to help you choose the right annuity for your retirement portfolio.

## *The Big Picture*

There are many investors who are willing to invest in long-term investments, but there are a few investors who are willing to invest in short-term investments. The latter do not mind watching their investments rise and fall on a regular basis. There are some investors, especially those who are nearing their retirement age, who cannot accept any short-term volatility in their portfolios. If you are an investor who has a moderate or low risk tolerance, you must choose to invest in an annuity.

### Points to Remember

Investors usually acquire annuities to create a steady stream of income for themselves during their retirement. The two major types of annuities you must consider are immediate and deferred annuities. The tax benefits offered by annuities include tax-deferred growth, but the amount you withdraw will be added to your income for the calculating your income tax. Most annuities levy a penalty on early withdrawals. The contract of annuity is formed between the insurance company and the annuitant or the investor. The insurance company offers to pay a specific sum of money for a specific period.

## *Tax Benefits of Annuities*

There are many tax benefits offered by an annuity. The earnings help you avoid paying out too much tax, especially during the accumulation phase of the annuity contract. You will only need to pay an income tax when you begin to withdraw money from the annuity.

If you use an IRA to contribute to the annuity, or any other tax-advantaged retirement account to transfer money to the annuity, you will be able to decrease your taxable income. This will help you save your contribution to the tax. Your tax savings will compound over a period of time and will help to boost your returns.

Additionally, you will not be able to predict when you will die. It is for this reason that the insurance company is only worried about your average retirement lifespan. It is very easy for the insurance company to predict the average lifespan of the clients. The insurer will only operate on certainty. It is for this reason that the insurance company will price the annuity marginally to ensure that it will retain more money when compared to the amount that it will need to payout to the clients. The client will still receive a certain income from the insurance company.

An annuity offers investors numerous provisions like a guaranteed number of years when payments will be made. If you, as the investor, die before the amounts are paid, the insurer will either pay the amount to the spouse, partner or the estate. The monthly payments will be smaller if the number of guarantees increase in the contract.

## Issues to Consider

When it comes to an overall retirement plan, it does make sense to include an annuity. Before you purchase an annuity, you must consider the following:

Are you only planning to invest in an annuity for a long-term goal or are you saving for your retirement? Are you choosing to invest in the annuity because you are looking for a tax-advantaged plan? If the answer to that is yes, you must realize that you will not be gaining any additional benefit?

When it comes to a variable annuity, will you be okay if the value of the account fell to a value that is below the amount that you had initially invested because the fund or the portfolio you invested in did not do well? Are you aware of the expenses and fees you will incur when you choose to invest in an annuity? Do you wish to hold the annuity for a long period so you can avoid paying any surrender charges when you choose to withdraw the money from the account? If you do withdraw money from the annuity, are you aware of how it will affect your tax liability?

## *The Bottom Line*

An annuity offers a growth that is tax deferred. This can result in a long-term return that will be significant. You must always contribute to the annuity for a lengthy period and only withdraw these funds once you retire. The tax benefits offered by a deferred annuity will always amount to substantial savings, and you will be at peace. You must always understand what you will gain from an annuity before you add it to your retirement profile.

# CHAPTER SEVEN

# HIGH-RISK INVESTMENT

If the type of investment you want to invest in offers a high rate of return within a short duration, it usually means that the investment is somewhat risky. With the right time, most of the investments can help double the principal of your investment. However, a lot of investors tend to opt for high-yield investments that expire within a short period even though the probability of risk on such investments is quite high. Please remember that there is no scientific formula you can follow to double your investment using any instrument. However, there are several instances wherein investments doubled in value within a short period. For every one of those investments that turned out exceptionally well, there are hundreds of investments that didn't go as planned. So, the burden of ensuring that you choose the right instrument rests on your shoulders.

There is a simple technique known as the rule of 72, which can be used for determining the time it will take for an investment to double given that its rate of interest stays fixed. When you divide the annual rate of return by 72, it will give you a rough estimate of how long it will take for the initial investment to at least double itself. For instance, if you are investing a dollar with an interest rate of 10% per annum, then it will take 7.2 years for the dollar to double itself (72 years/10= 7.2 years). So, if you have the time and patience, then you can use this rule to double your money.

## Invest in Options

Options certainly offer a high rate of return on investment. When you purchase an option, you have an offer to purchase an underlying stock or commodity at a given price at a specific time in the future. If the price of the security increases during its maturity, then you can decide to purchase or sell the security. However, if the value of the commodities doesn't increase as desired, the investor doesn't have to purchase the securities. This is quite a risky form of investment because the purchase or the sale of securities needs to be finalized within a specific period.

The advantage of investing in an option is that you are given the chance of acquiring stocks at a nominal value and then wait for their value to increase before paying for them in full. If the value of the option doesn't increase, then you lose the advance you put down, and nothing more than that. It is a high-risk investment, and therefore the returns on it are high as well. When done correctly, an investor can acquire this instrument for a low price and sell it when the price increases for earning a profit. Options are quite flexible and can work well with any method of trading.

The disadvantage of this instrument is that the stock prices don't usually fluctuate drastically, whereas the value of options does. If speculation isn't your forte, then you must stay away from options. These investments are risk capital investments, and this means that the capital you invest in this instrument is risky, and it can swing either way for you. You might get the opportunity to earn a profit or even lose your capital. Once the period lapses, the option expires, and it becomes worthless.

## Securitization

Securitization is the process of creating a financial instrument by combining different financial assets and then marketing these different tiers of securities to investors, and this process can comprise of different types of financial assets, and it also helps to promote liquidity in the market. Securities that are backed by mortgage will be a perfect instance of securitization. By clubbing up the mortgages, the issuer can then divide this huge pool into smaller parts based on the risk of default of each of these individual mortgages and then resell these smaller portions to the investors.

This process helps to create liquidity by letting the smaller investors acquire shares that form a part of the more prominent asset pool. Making use of mortgage-backed securities, the individual investor can purchase a part of the mortgage as a kind of bond. Without securitization, the individual investor might not be able to afford to buy into the bigger pool of mortgages present. The company that is holding the loans is referred to as the originator, and they will gather the necessary data on different assets that it will take out from their related balance sheets. These assets will then be gathered together based on factors like the period remaining on loan, the risk involved, and so on. This group of assets that have been gathered together will then be sold to an issuer. The issuer will then create a set of tradable securities representing a stake in the associated assets and will, in turn, sell the same to investors who are interested at a special rate.

Securitization will provide the creditors with a means of lowering the associated risks through the dissection of the ownership of the obligations of debt. The investors will assume the position of a lender by purchasing the security. The investor can earn a return that is based on the principle of association and the payments towards interests that are made by the debtors under their obligation. Unlike other forms of investments, this particular type of investment is based on tangible goods. In case of a default in payment by the debtor, then the underlying asset can be seized and sold for compensating for the default in payment. Like with any other investment, the higher the risk involved, the higher will be the potential of returns on it.

## Exchange-Traded Commodity or ETCs

Exchange traded commodities are referred to as ETCs, and they give the trader and the investor exposure to commodities via shares. These are traded like a stock, which is they are traded on a stock exchange. ETCs track the movement of the price of the underlying commodity like oil, silver and even gold and their prices will fluctuate depending on the value of these underlying commodities. ETCs can track individual commodities or even a basket of commodities. For instance, an ETC basket will be an instrument that will track multiple metals instead of one or it can even track different agricultural commodities like wheat, soybeans, and corn. The structure of the ETCs can vary depending on the issuing company. There are individual exchanges around the world like the London stock exchange and the Australian Securities Exchange that will offer ETCs with a specific structure. These ETCs will track the price of the commodity. There will be a management fee that will be charged, and this will be the compensation for the company that's running these instruments. ETCs will provide a net asset value, and this is the fair value of an ETC. The commodity market can be a physical or a virtual marketplace for trading in the commodities. There are about 50 commodity markets that are present around the world, and there are about 100 commodities that are traded on them. The commodities can be categorized as hard and soft commodities. Natural resources that can be mined or extracted like gold, rubber, and oil will be examples of hard commodities. Soft commodities, on the other hand, will be agricultural products or even livestock like corn, wheat, pork, and so on.

There are different ways in which you can invest in commodities. The stock can be purchased in those corporations whose business is dependent on commodity prices or even invest in mutual funds or ETFs that focus on companies related to commodities. The direct way of investing in these investments will be by buying a futures contract. A future contract will place an obligation of buying or selling the commodity at a specific price on the date of delivery sometime in the future. The major commodity exchanges in the US are located in Chicago and New York.

## Hedge Fund

A hedge fund is an alternative type of investment that pools together the capital obtained from different individual or institutional investors and invests that capital in different assets to build a diverse portfolio and effectively manage the risks. Hedge funds tend to invest in various types of varied investments ranging from real estate, to commodities, and to available alternative assets. This is one of the primary differences between a hedge fund and a mutual fund, which normally restricts its investments to stocks or bonds. The goal of a hedge fund is to maximize the returns to an investor while reducing and hedging the risk regardless of whether the market's health is up or down. Hedge funds became rather popular during the streak of bullish markets in the US economy in the 1920's before the great depression. At present, hedge funds are valued at several trillions of dollars.

Hedge funds are usually perceived to be quite an aggressive and risky form of investment, especially when compared with the more conservative options available in the market. The investment strategy followed differs from one hedge fund to another, but the idea of all the hedge funds is the same- to use trading techniques that help to hedge their bets and prevent any losses to their clients. The success of a hedge fund essentially depends on the ability of the hedge fund manager to anticipate any changes in the market and react in a suitable manner.

Hedge funds tend to invest in a variety of investment options ranging from real estate, to currencies, to alternative assets and everything else in between. Since hedge funds are privately owned, they are free to do as they please with the funds as long as they are being upfront with their clients. This degree of leniency toward the hedge fund manager makes the investment quite risky. Essentially, your chances of earning a profit or incurring a loss are dependent on the hedge fund manager's ability to think and make decisions. However, this does also give this investment a lot of flexibility.

## Structured Products

Structured products have been designed for facilitating customized risk-return goals. This is made possible by taking any regular security like the conventional bond and then replacing the usual features of payments with a couple of unconventional payoffs that are derived not from the cash flow of the issuer, but the performance of the underlying assets. The return on these investments will depend on the performance of the underlying assets. If the return on the underlying asset is "x," then the payout on the structured product will be "y." This will mean that the performance of the structured product will be related to the traditional model of option pricing, even though they might contain other types of derivatives like swaps, forwards, and even futures as well as several embedded features like downside buffers. Structured products had become popular in the European markets, and they have gained popularity in the US as well. In the US, they are made available as products registered with the SEC. This means that they will be available to investors in the same manner as stocks, bonds, ETFs, and even mutual funds. These investments can offer customized exposure to usually hard to reach classes and subclasses of assets that will make these structured products a useful component of a diversified portfolio.

Let us look at an example to get a better understanding of how these instruments function. For instance, a big bank has issued these structured products in the form of notes where each of these notes has a face value of $1000. Each note will be a package that will comprise two components like a zero-coupon bond and a call option on the underlying instrument, like the common stock or an ETF that will mimic a popular index like the S&P 500 with a maturity period of three years. The pricing of this instrument will be complex. However, the principle involved is quite simple. On the date of issue, you will have to pay the face value, which is $1000 per note. This will be a principal protected investment, which means you will get the $1000 you have invested on maturity regardless of what will happen to the underlying asset. Now, let us look at the performance aspect of this instrument. Let us assume that the underlying asset happens to be a European call option. The return you will earn will depend on the value of the investment at the date of its maturity. If this happens to be higher than the issuing value, then in such a case, you will earn a profit in addition to the original principal. However, if the option is worthless on the date of expiration, you will receive your original principal without any additions to it. This means you will get your $1000 back on maturity.

In the previous example, the key feature is the protection of the principal. In a different situation, the investor might be willing to trade all or some of this protection offered in favor of a performance feature, which is more attractive. Consider another scenario. The investor wants to trade off the principal protection for a combination of other performance features.

A common risk that all structure products possess will be the lack of liquidity due to the customized nature of these investments. Until the date of the maturity, the full return from this investment cannot be realized. This is the reason because of which the structured products tend to be an investment decision that goes along the lines of "buy and hold." Apart from liquidity, the other risk associated with this form of investment will be the credit quality of the issuer. The cash flow is derived from other sources; the product on its own is considered to be the liability of the financial institution that is issuing it. Also, there is no transparency in pricing strategies.

That is, there is no uniform pricing standard for these investments. This will be difficult for making a comparison of different structured offerings.

## Angel Investor

The term angel investor is used to denote a private investor who offers finance and support a business requires during its initial stages. Becoming an angel investor is quite a risky option since you need to have a sense of business acumen along with basic knowledge about the business you want to get involved in. Angel investors are usually offered shares, or any other form of security of the business that represents debt, equity, or a combination of the two. They are also referred to as business angels. In the past, angel investors were often entrepreneurs who exited their business and wanted to help newcomers get a foothold in the industry by mentoring them and helping them raise the necessary capital for their business ventures. Angel investors are usually involved in the business during its conception and inception stages. These are the first outsiders who get effectively involved in a business.

So, what are the different benefits an investor can get? Well, the risk taken by an angel investor is rather significant and high. Therefore, the returns offered on this type of investment are high too. If you are looking for a significant payout, then this is a good option. In some countries, an angel investor is also eligible for certain tax concessions. For instance, in the UK, an angel investor can claim tax reliefs according to the Seed Enterprise Investment Scheme and the Enterprise Investment Scheme. If you have good ideas and are knowledgeable about your chosen niche, then you can always offer advice to the business you invest in. Apart from this, it is a great way to increase your business network and create a name for yourself as an angel investor in the market.

However, there are certain risks associated with becoming an angel investor. The first and the most obvious risk of all is the fact that investing in a startup is a risky gamble. When it comes to startups, the concept of taking calculated risks doesn't exist. Even if the idea sounds lovely to you, there is no guarantee that the startup will be successful. If the business goes into a loss, then your investment can be lost! If you want to become an angel investor, another thing you must consider is the time taken to earn your returns. It might offer high returns, but to earn such high returns, you must stay in the game for longer. A lot of people seem to think that they can exit the game after maybe three to five years, but ideally, you must stay in the game for ten years to earn excellent returns, provided everything goes favorably and as planned.

# CONCLUSION

I want to thank you for choosing this book. I hope it proved to be an informative and enjoyable read.

By now, you will have realized that attaining your financial dream is a practical goal. However, to attain that goal, you need some time, effort, and the right resources. Armed with the information given in this book, you can achieve the financial freedom you always desired.

The first step toward attaining your financial goals is to analyze your current financial status, decide your goals, and then make a plan of action to attain those goals. There are different types of investment options you can utilize. According to your financial capacity, the risks involved, and the returns you expect, you need to identify the best possible investment options. Apart from this, you must also consider budgeting and creating an emergency fund to ensure that you always have the finances you need.

Now, all that's left for you to do is get started and the take the first step toward budgeting and investing.

Thank you and all the best!